ENDORSEMENTS

4 Cycles of Revival is a timely and essential guide for anyone who is hungry not only to experience God's presence but to understand and steward it with wisdom. My friend, pastor, and prophetic voice of this hour, Todd Smith, who has faithfully led and stewarded the North Georgia Revival, brings rare clarity to the often misunderstood seasons that follow powerful encounters, helping believers navigate both the fire and the refining.

I am so excited for this book. It offers profound insight into the depth and dynamics of true moves of God. With pastoral insight and prophetic depth, this book equips readers to recognize where they are in God's movement and respond with maturity and purpose. This book is for every pastor who wants to understand the processes of revival and lead with greater clarity and confidence. It challenges complacency while offering hope, reminding us that every phase of revival carries divine intention: *"To everything there is a season, a time for every purpose under heaven"* (Ecclesiastes 3:1 NKJV). This is more than a book; it is a road map for sustaining what God ignites. A must-read for leaders and believers who refuse to let revival fade prematurely.

Pat Schatzline
Evangelist, Author, and Entrepreneur
Remnant Ministries International
Fort Worth, Texas

What I know about the author of this book is that every book I have read from him has touched me deeply within my spirit. The truth and knowledge behind every word come straight from his heart. A man who, in my eyes, is one of the most humble men I have ever met. He is truly an inspiration to all those who get to read what he writes and glean from his life and knowledge of serving God!

Pastor Jason Abney
Life of Love Ministry Center
Martinsville, Trafalgar, Indiana

If you're in a move of God, or hungry for one, I encourage you to get Pastor Todd's book, *4 Cycles of Revival.* I believe few have been able to sustain and steward a move of God as effectively or with the longevity as what God has been pouring out at the North Georgia Revival for more than eight years now. The insight and wisdom Pastor Todd has gleaned will help you ignite and sustain the fire that God needs His Church to be.

Pastor Tim Lunk
Emmanuel Church
Vinita, Oklahoma

Pastor Todd's stewardship of the North Georgia Revival has positively impacted me and our church and has encouraged us to carry the flame of revival for our region! This book will help pastors and leaders steward and sustain a move of God and will help every believer in maintaining perseverance and longevity to help them run their race and finish well.

Jeff Freeman
Senior Pastor, The Altar Church
Joplin, Missouri

Learning to steward the seasons of the believer's journey is essential to experiencing the fullness of what God desires to do. This powerful and timely book equips pastors, leaders, and spiritually hungry believers to recognize and respond to moments of divine opportunity. Drawing from the insight of a present-day revival leader, this is more than a book—it's a guide to cultivating lasting revival in your life and church.

Pastor Jason Murphy
Reach Church
White Plains, New York

4 Cycles of Revival is, without question, one of the most transformative literary tools in my personal and ministerial life. The revelatory keys within these pages have empowered me to not only understand moves of God but to accurately discern the seasons of ministry and the ebbs and flows of church growth. The wisdom in this book is truly priceless!

Pastor David Edmondson
Covenant Connections Church
Flowery Branch, Georgia

4 Cycles of Revival is a prophetic road map for the body of Christ in this hour, bringing clarity to the divine rhythms that follow powerful encounters with God and revealing that what many perceive as silence or struggle is often the sanctifying work of the Spirit preparing us to carry greater glory. With piercing insight, Todd Smith calls believers beyond chasing moments into stewarding sustained moves of God, positioning hungry hearts not only to experience revival but to endure, mature, and faithfully carry what He is releasing.

David Sorrels
Lead Pastor, Gateway Church International
York, Pennsylvania

Todd Smith's book, *4 Cycles to Revival*, taught me life lessons about hosting revival. It showed me that storms will also come with a move of God, and not to give up.

Pastor Dan Goostree
The Gathering Tabernacle
Rocky Comfort, Missouri

Throughout the ages, believers have cried out these words in prayer, "Oh Lord, send revival and pour out your Spirit again." There are countless stories of great things God has done, and questions about why they ended. In Pastor Todd Smith's new book, *4 Cycles of Revival*, he takes the pulse of past revivals and brings clarity to the revival process. What I personally learned was that God moves in cycles, not circles! What we see as stumbling blocks are actually stepping stones! I highly recommend this book to all who want to partner with God in the final harvest.

Pastor Larry Rocquin
Grace Church of Paulina, Louisiana
Leader of the Southeast Louisiana Revival

This book is a must for anyone seeking revival! When you give God your yes, understanding these cycles will be vital to help sustain any move of God. All moves of God come with a cost; this book will help you navigate through the cycles and steward the gift of God's glory!

Pastor Allen Weileng
Harvest Church
Freeport, Minnesota

This book packs a powerful punch. It presents a compelling call to authentic, sustained revival, grounded in truth and filled with Spirit-led insight. Revival is more than words; it is a life shaped by prayer and obedience to God's Word, which Pastor Todd consistently exemplifies. His teaching in *4 Cycles of Revival* offers clear, practical wisdom for leaders who are hungry to see revival touch this generation and beyond.

Pastor Jorge Figueroa
Church of the Sower
Orlando, Florida

4 CYCLES OF REVIVAL

DESTINY IMAGE BOOKS BY TODD SMITH

Unless We Pray: The Hour Is Late. God Has a Plan and This Is It!

Creating a Habitation for God's Glory

Igniting Revival Fire Every Day

4 Cycles of Revival

4 CYCLES OF REVIVAL

How to Recognize, Respond to, and Engage with God During Seasons of Divine Encounters

TODD SMITH

 All emphasis within Scripture quotations is the author's own. Take note that the name satan and related names are not capitalized. We choose not to acknowledge him, even to the point of violating grammatical rules.

DESTINY IMAGE® PUBLISHERS, INC.
P.O. Box 310, Shippensburg, PA 17257-0310
"Publishing cutting-edge prophetic resources to supernaturally empower the body of Christ"

This book and all other Destiny Image and Destiny Image Fiction books are available at Christian bookstores and distributors worldwide.

For more information on foreign distributors, call 717-532-3040.
Reach us on the Internet: www.destinyimage.com.

ISBN 13 TP: 979-8-8815-0949-1
ISBN 13 eBook: 979-8-8815-0950-7

For Worldwide Distribution, Printed in the U.S.A.
1 2 3 4 5 6 7 8 / 30 29 28 27 26

CONTENTS

FOREWORD

Every single church—and every Christian life—can live in revival.

Bold promise? No. It's an invitation. But it's not a call to continuous excitement. It's an invitation to live like the sons of Issachar of old and recognize what the Holy Spirit is doing in your church, your ministry, and your personal life in every season and cycle of revival.

Too many people assume revival looks like one thing, and when that one expression of revival ceases, they conclude the move of God is dead. And alas, this is precisely why moves of God have gone dormant throughout history—not because God stopped moving, but because He shifted. The cloud and the fire moved. A different cycle started. A new season was entered. And rather than truly wanting God and what God wants, we fell in love. Not with revival itself, but with a specific *season* of revival—and that season became our preference. So much so that we were unwilling to partner with the Spirit's movement as He called us into the new. Into the next. Into advancement. Into maturity. Into a life that *carries* the spirit of revival rather than merely *enjoys* it.

We have been Peter on the mountain, asking to build three tabernacles to preserve a single moment of glory, when Jesus was already walking back down the mountain to do the next thing.

This is the gift of Pastor Todd Smith's new book.

Without exaggeration, I believe this is one of the top five books every pastor needs—and every Christian should read—on the subject of revival. It comes from a practitioner, not from an ivory-tower theorist offering opinions about what revival *should* look like from a safe distance. Todd writes from inside the fire. The North Georgia Revival is not a case study he researched; it is a furnace he has stewarded—through the breathtaking days of Stimulation, the costly refining of Sanctification, the trembling weight of Shock and Awe, and the disciplined deployment of Service.

I met Todd Smith in the Jordan River in 2019. I'm sure we had pleasant exchanges before that, but it was during a Sid Roth tour to Israel—with three to four hundred people present—that we became fast friends. Todd was facilitating water baptisms in the Jordan, and I was serving as one of the leaders helping to baptize. There, on that ancient river, we experienced a manifestation of the electric power of God—the same power that has been touching tens of thousands of lives in the baptismal waters in Dawsonville. I have not merely heard about this move; I have stood in it. And I tell you: the man writing this book has been entrusted with something rare, and he has refused to loosen his grip.

That matters because what you hold in your hands is not theory. It is testimony with a teaching ministry attached to it. Todd will warn you with the lessons of Azusa—that revival rarely dies from outside opposition; it weakens because the people carrying it were not yet prepared for the responsibility that came with it. He will sober you with the truth that what God births in power must be stewarded with wisdom. He will press you, gently but unmistakably, toward the kind of maturity that can carry glory without crushing under it.

This book will cause your heart to burn for revival, yes. But it will also position you to recognize what the Spirit of God is actually doing in *your* season—and to partner with His movement and activity, no matter in which cycle you find yourself.

Dutch Sheets says it simply, but brilliantly: "When you know what time it is, you know what to do."

This book will show you what time it is in God's movement. And once you know, you will know how to partner with the Holy Spirit to receive every blessing and every benefit of that unique cycle of revival.

The fire that God is releasing in this hour will not be carried by spectators. It will be carried by sons and daughters of Issachar—discerning the times, refusing to loosen their grip, willing to take off their shoes when the season changes, and willing to be deployed when the Lord finally says, *Go.*

Read this book slowly. Read it prayerfully. And then do what Todd has done. *Live it*.

Larry Sparks
Revivalist, Vice President of Publishing for Nori Media Group
MDiv., Church History and Renewal, Regent University
Bestselling Author of *Pentecostal Fire*

FOREWORD

Revival. It is the deep longing of every heart that truly loves Jesus and His presence. We pray for it. We pursue it. We cry out for God to reveal His presence, His power, and His glory in ways that are tangible and life-changing. And then—whether by His sovereignty or in response to a hungry people—He comes.

That is exactly what happened to us at Christ Fellowship Church in Dawsonville, Georgia, in 2018. The God of heaven began to manifest His glory among us and has continued to do so for more than seven years now.

Having never experienced revival on this level, we did not fully understand what it would require—or what it would bring. Yes, the miracles came. Healing and deliverance came. Salvation, restoration, signs, and wonders—they came in abundance. But revival did not come alone.

Almost overnight, thousands of people began arriving—from across the United States and around the world. They heard how Jesus was meeting people in the baptism waters, and they came to encounter Jesus for themselves. Long lines formed as people waited to step into the water, believing for transformation. Every night carried weight—needs that were deep, urgent, and at times life-threatening.

And with this outpouring came an equally weighty responsibility, long hours of ministry and constant serving. There was also the ongoing care of people and the stewardship of a growing and stretched environment. There were practical demands—facility needs, financial pressures, organizational challenges—all while continuing to shepherd our own church family.

We were caught up in something undeniably powerful, yet we had to learn, in real time, how to navigate everything that revival brings. Revival isn't always understood or embraced. It can be confusing, exhausting, disruptive, and unpredictable. Simply put—revival creates a swirl.

And we found ourselves in the swirl.

Very early on, we were faced with questions we did not yet have answers for because we had never seen anything like this. Things took off so fast in the beginning—we were wondering, *What's happening?* Other questions arose. Why does revival feel different from one moment to the next? How do we sustain this? Where is the balance? Why does passion surge one season and seem to wane in another? Why does God feel so near at times—and so quiet at others? How do we keep going when we are exhausted?

What we came to understand is this: *revival moves in cycles.*

There are moments of *stimulation*—when the presence of God is overwhelming, the atmosphere is charged with faith, and miracles flow with undeniable power. Expectation builds, and everything feels alive with the activity of heaven. Everyone loves this initial phase!

Then comes *sanctification*—when God turns His light inward. He begins to refine, correct, and purify, searching the heart as He prepares His people to carry what He is doing. This season is often uncomfortable, but it is essential.

There are also seasons of *shock and awe*—when God moves in ways that defy expectation and stretch every category. His power and presence overwhelm understanding. These are the moments that leave you undone, marked by the undeniable reality that God is in your midst.

And then there is *service*—the often unseen, demanding, day-after-day work of ministry. The crowds still come, and the needs are fierce. In this cycle, revival is sustained not by emotion, but by faithfulness. It is here that endurance is formed, and prayer is the fuel.

These cycles do not move in a straight line, nor do they exist in isolation. Each one is necessary. Each one is used by God to build, refine, strengthen, and prepare His people. They overlap, repeat, and unfold in ways that can feel unpredictable. *Without understanding them, revival can begin to feel overwhelming—even unsustainable.* But when you understand that revival moves in cycles, and you understand how to move through each cycle, you are less likely to quit when things get challenging and more likely to remain faithful and steady.

After years of walking through these cycles (and as cycles do, they repeat), Todd has gained invaluable insight into how to navigate each one—how to recognize it, how to respond to it, and how to remain steady within it. What he shares is not theory. It has been lived and tested. It is essential for anyone who desires not only to experience revival, but to sustain it.

Revival does not have to end. In truth, it should not. But often, it does—not because God stops moving, but because people are unprepared for what revival requires. When fatigue sets in, when passion wanes, when challenges arise, many do not know how to remain. Discouragement can take root, and without clarity and understanding of the flow of revival, many step away.

This book changes that.

It gives language to the experience and clarity to the swirl. It equips you to stand—so that what God begins can continue, and many more can encounter the transforming power of His presence.

I was so thankful when I first heard Todd teach on *4 Cycles of Revival*. I remember thinking, *Thank You, Jesus! Finally, I get it. Everyone needs to hear and understand this!* Now you, too, can understand that revival is *demanding,* and you will go through *cycles* of change over and over, but it won't kill you. Each one has a purpose!

In Proverbs 4:7, the Bible says, *"Wisdom is the principal thing; therefore get wisdom. And with all your getting, get understanding"* (NKJV). This book will help you understand the revival cycles—showing you not only how to endure the seasons of revival, but how to recognize them, steward them, and even find joy in them.

I am grateful for this revelatory teaching, and I am excited for you to journey through these pages for yourself. Because of this book, you will never be caught off guard by *the cycles of revival,* but rather you will be equipped with understanding to finish strong!

Karen Smith, PhD

Doctorate of Ministries, President of KINEO Ministry

Training Center, Dawsonville, Georgia

PART ONE

UNDERSTANDING THE CYCLES

1

THE GLORY OF GOD

In the early days of the Azusa Street Revival (1906), something unexpected happened. The fire department showed up. Someone had reported flames coming from the roof of a rundown building on Azusa Street in Los Angeles. Neighbors swore they saw fire. They were not wrong, but the building was not burning. Heaven had come down.

The *Los Angeles Times* even covered the strange events. Crowds stood outside trying to figure out what was happening inside the dilapidated former stable at 312 Azusa Street.[1]

What they were witnessing wasn't smoke.

It was glory.

When revival touches the earth there are many wonderful events and emotions that take place in the space of visitation. For starters, there is an incessant conscious awareness of the nearness of God. God becomes the centerpiece of everyday life. You feel Him, sense Him in everything you do.

Within Christian circles we are hearing more and more about the glory of God. Why the shift? Why suddenly are Christian leaders speaking on the significance and splendor of the glory of God?

Throughout the ages people have tried to articulate what the glory of God is. It is hard to accurately define, but it is nearly impossible to forget after a person encounters it.

THE ATMOSPHERE SHIFTS

I have witnessed the glory of God many times during the North Georgia Revival, and every encounter has been unique and life-altering. No two moments have felt the same. Each time His presence intensifies in the room, each time He chooses to manifest His nearness, it carries weight and depth that cannot be manufactured or explained. Something shifts within us. A holy metamorphosis begins. A deeper hunger for Jesus awakens in the hearts of those present. It feels as though the entire room undergoes a baptism in His splendor and awe.

Revival has taught me that God never moves in monotone or simple black-and-white shades. His work is far more beautiful and diverse than that. Yes, His presence is simple, but it is never simplistic; there is otherworld complexity to it. Not all encounters with His glory are the same. His glory carries layers, depths, and dimensions, but every encounter with it redirects a person's life—I know it has mine.

The Hebrew word for *glory* is *kabod*. At its core, *kabod* means weight, heaviness, substance. It describes not merely the beauty of God, but the gravity of His presence. When the glory of God fills a room, it is not just emotional or atmospheric—it is substantial. It presses upon the human body with holy significance, reminding us that we are standing before Someone infinitely real, infinitely holy, and infinitely worthy.

HEAVEN'S NEARNESS

The best way I can describe the glory of God is this: it feels a lot like humidity.

Here in the Deep South, Georgia in particular, we know humidity well. Down here, humidity doesn't politely introduce itself. It doesn't knock. It just walks in and hugs you. One step outside and your glasses fog up, your hair starts negotiating with gravity, and you suddenly understand why "sweet tea" exists in gallon containers.

You don't have to be told humidity is present, you feel it instantly. It clings to you. It wraps around you. There are days when the air is so thick you can feel it pressing against your body. It affects you. It changes how you move, how you breathe, even how long you plan to stay outside.

This is the closest natural picture I know of what Scripture describes when the glory of God fills a place.

When Solomon dedicated the temple in 2 Chronicles 7, the glory of God filled the house so powerfully that the priests could not even stand to minister. The weight of His presence made normal activity impossible.

In the same way, when God's glory fills a room, it becomes unmistakable, tangible, and deeply experiential. The very atmosphere seems to change. Breathing feels different. Movement becomes limited, sometimes voluntarily, as hearts bow in reverence, and sometimes involuntarily, as people find themselves overwhelmed by the nearness of God.

The prophet Ezekiel tried to describe what he saw and experienced by the River Chebar:

> *And above the firmament over their heads was the likeness of a throne…from the appearance of His waist and upward I saw, as it were, the color of amber with the appearance of fire all around….*
> *…Like the appearance of a rainbow in a cloud on a rainy day, so was the appearance of the brightness all around it. This was the appearance of the likeness of the glory of the Lord. So when I saw it, I fell on my face…* (Ezekiel 1:26-28 NKJV).

Later, he encountered that same glory again: "*…the glory of the Lord stood there, like the glory which I saw by the River Chebar; and I fell on my face*" (Ezekiel 3:23 NKJV).

Notice the pattern. Every time the glory of God appears in Scripture, one common reality emerges—it becomes difficult to function as normal. Human strength gives way to holy awe. Physical capacity yields to divine presence.

Why?

Because the human heart and body are being overwhelmed by the radiance of God's presence, the absolute perfection of untainted holiness.

When the glory comes, everything changes.

2

A WARNING FROM AZUSA

I want to continue to look into the Azusa Street Revival.

A few years ago, I stood at 214 North Bonnie Brae Street in Los Angeles, California. As I stood there quietly, I tried to imagine the bustling activity that once filled that modest home more than a century ago. The anticipation. The hunger. The awe. The unmistakable joy of people encountering the presence of God.

I must admit I was stricken by the moment. It was here at this very spot that a move of God was birthed, called the Azusa Street Revival. This revival stands as one of the most consequential moves of God in modern church history. What began in obscurity became the catalyst for the modern Pentecostal movement, reshaping global Christianity in a matter of months.

And like every authentic move of God, it began quietly. There were no famous preachers, charisma, or strategic plans in place. Instead, the early days were marked by the same ingredients that have birthed revivals throughout history. Humility. Brokenness. Prayer. Repentance. And a desperation for God.[2]

Under the leadership of William J. Seymour, a humble African-American preacher, the revival became known for something almost unheard of in early 20th century America—racial unity. People from every social class, background, and ethnicity gathered together to seek God.

INSIDE A CRATE

Eyewitnesses described Seymour frequently praying with his head inside a wooden crate, intentionally hiding his face so that no attention would fall upon him. His desire was simple: Christ alone would be exalted.[3]

The atmosphere was said to be marked by reverence and repentance. Many fell to their knees in fear and spontaneously confessed their sins. There was a profound awareness of God's holiness. It was raw and unpolished, but undeniably real.

WHEN REVIVAL EXPLODES

The growth of the revival was explosive and quick. As word of this revival fire spread, people began traveling from across the United States and around the world to witness what God was doing in Los Angeles. When they arrived, they were not disappointed. God met them and changed them.

As a result, numerous people were saved and baptized with the Holy Spirit. Many spoke in tongues. Others testified of miraculous healings. The atmosphere was electric with the presence of God. In addition, missionaries were sent out rapidly. Denominations were birthed, and Pentecostal theology spread globally.[4] Within just a few years, the influence of Azusa Street spread across America and to nations around the world.

Historians widely agree that the modern global Pentecostal movement, which now numbers hundreds of millions of believers, traces its roots back to what happened in that house.

SOMETHING ELSE WAS HAPPENING

Yet beneath the outward explosion of revival, something else was taking place, something quieter and far more dangerous. The growth of the movement began to outpace the capacity of the people leading it.

Revival historian Vinson Synan wrote in his book, "*As crowds increased, pressures multiplied. Competing voices emerged. Doctrinal extremes found room to grow.*"[5] Cecil M. Robeck Jr., a church historian, adds, "Personal ambition crept in where humility once governed. Racial tensions, once miraculously overcome, resurfaced. Leadership became strained under the weight of expectations that far exceeded the structure and discipleship capacity of the movement."

What had once been a revival centered on God's presence slowly became fragmented by controversy, competing visions, and personality conflicts. Seymour, once the unifying spiritual father of the movement, found himself marginalized. The very humility, hunger, and passion that birthed the revival was no longer universally shared among those now stewarding its influence. Something had shifted.

THE ENEMY'S SMALL OPENING

This small opening was all the devil needed. The devil rarely destroys a revival in a single dramatic moment. More often, he simply looks for small cracks in the foundation. His goal was to diminish the influence of the Azusa Street revival and bring it to a premature close. However, the fire did not go out instantly. But it flickered and was weakened.

What lesson(s) can we learn? The problem was not power. The problem was not a lack of God's presence—both were present and on full display. The main issue was stewardship. In my opinion, the collapse was not due to doctrinal disputes, persecution from the outside, or the negative assessments of media and the religious community. All of those things were present, but it was not as obvious as indicated; it was something hidden, more sinister, more private. The pressure came from the inside—people and personalities adding their opinion or insight as to what should happen next. This is not uncommon with moves of God, and before we become too critical, it is human nature that tries to improve what is in front of us. But revival rarely survives human control.

Frank Bartleman noted: "At the beginning of the revival the emphasis was wholly on God. Men were hidden and Christ was exalted. But gradually the Spirit was grieved, and human control began to replace divine guidance. Organization took the place of the

Spirit's leadership, and the glory that once filled the meetings began to fade. We still held the services, but the depth of the presence was not the same. The form of revival remained, but the fire that had birthed it was slowly withdrawing."[6]

THE REAL LESSON OF AZUSA

As with Azuza and any other move of God, there is a steep learning curve. Azusa teaches us that revival can survive outside pressure, persecution, and negative press, but it struggles to survive immaturity. When God pours out His Spirit upon a people, He does not override the human equation. Instead, He entrusts human beings with the responsibility of stewarding what He has birthed. That is a sacred and dangerous responsibility.

At Azusa, the revival advanced faster than the leaders themselves were formed. The spiritual weight placed upon them eventually exceeded their capacity to carry it.

The revival did not fail because God stopped moving. It weakened because the people carrying it were not yet fully prepared for the responsibility that came with it.

THE WARNING FOR EVERY REVIVAL

In the beginning of a revival no one is fully prepared to carry it at its most weighty position. This is why maturity must grow alongside revival. The greater the outpouring, the greater the stewardship required.

History is filled with examples of revivals that began in extraordinary power but ended prematurely because the people carrying them were not prepared for the weight of what God had entrusted to them.

And that raises a sobering question for every generation: If God were to send revival today, would we be ready to carry it?

3

THAT IS A LOT OF BABIES!

According to the *World Population Review,* every single day the world welcomes more than 362,000 newborn babies. That translates to roughly 15,000 births every hour, 252 every minute, and four precious lives every second.[7] By the end of the year, more than 130,000,000 children will have entered the world. The numbers are staggering.

Surprisingly, the same research shows that India leads all nations with over 63,000 births each day. Wow, that's a lot of babies! In contrast, the United States welcomes just over 10,000 newborns daily, while among industrialized nations, South Korea now records the lowest birth rate in the world, with only 673 births per day.[8]

One thing is certain: life is constantly being born. Yet no one believes that birth alone guarantees a healthy, prosperous future. Each one of those precious children enters the world fragile, vulnerable, dependent, and unfinished. Each child needs care, oversight, guidance, protection, and nourishment. All of us would agree that healthy growth is not accidental and maturity is not automatic.

The same is true spiritually. And the same is true of revival.

Your new birth into the kingdom of God is just as delicate as a newborn entering the world. You have been miraculously born again, and now begins your adventurous new journey of loving and following the Jesus who saved you. Maturity is a process developed over time. Growth is not automatic—it must be intentional, nurtured, and protected.

Scripture never assumes that spiritual life will mature on its own. In fact, it repeatedly warns that without intentional growth, believers can remain immature, vulnerable, and unprepared for responsibility. For this reason, your spiritual development and maturity must become one of your highest aims. Failure to do so directly impacts not only you but those around you.

This book exists to help you understand how spiritual life grows, matures, and survives the changing seasons of God. Because what God births in power must be stewarded with wisdom.

Therefore, we must be proactive and nourish ourselves through the Word of God, submission to the Holy Spirit, prayer, and fellowship with other believers.

Spiritual maturity can be complicated, and it requires patience. Why? Because depth is formed slowly, often in hidden seasons when little seems to be happening. Just as a child grows through stages, so does the believer, learning obedience, humility, discernment, and endurance one step at a time. Maturity must be chosen, pursued, and protected. And when the believer makes growth a priority, they become capable of stewarding not only their own faith, but the weight of what God desires to do through them.

Hosting a move of God is similar. Every significant move of God begins with breathtaking power, and almost every move of God eventually fades. Not because God stopped moving. Not because God changed His mind. But because His people did not understand what came next.

When a church experiences revival, the revival does not sustain itself automatically. Like a newborn, revival requires careful attention, selfless leadership, and spiritual wisdom to navigate the changing seasons. What God births in a moment must be protected over time. It needs to be parented well. If mishandled, ignored, or taken for granted, what began with promise can weaken, stall, or even die prematurely.

History proves this sobering reality: many revivals were born powerfully but never fully matured. Not because God withdrew, but because His people underestimated what it takes to raise what heaven releases. As with children, it is not the moment of birth that determines the outcome; it is how the life is cared for in the days, months, and seasons that follow.

As stated previously, revival rarely dies in public moments. It fades quietly in the hidden seasons that follow the excitement. When the crowds thin, when the emotions settle, and when the spotlight moves on, what remains must be nurtured. The greatest threat to a move of God is not opposition, it is misunderstandings that lead to neglect.

This is why understanding the cycles of revival is not optional. It is essential. Because what God births in purity must be stewarded with humility, wisdom, and endurance, or the very thing we fasted and prayed for can quietly fade before it ever fulfills its purpose.

Our spiritual growth matters because revival cannot be sustained by immaturity. What God births in power must be carried by people who have and are being molded into His image. Let me put it this way: what begins in power must be sustained by intentional formation—not to control or dominate, or replace, but to oversee its health. If this is absent, the very revival God birthed will collapse under its own weight.

How a child is nurtured, parented, and cared for, especially through vulnerable transitions, will profoundly shape who they become and what they contribute to the world. In my opinion, neglect is the major contributor to underdevelopment. In the natural, uninvolved parenting can lead to poor self-esteem and social skills.[9]

The same is true in the spiritual. People who are not nurtured properly never become healthy spiritually. The transition through seasons shapes who they become and what they accomplish for the kingdom of God. The goal is for every believer to grow, mature, and fulfill their purpose. But this is not automatic.

4

CYCLES NOT CIRCLES

Have you ever noticed that the unhealthiest foods in a grocery store seem to have the most colorful packaging?

It is not accidental. Color speaks. The human brain is hardwired to notice bright colors; in fact, color primes the brain for pleasure. Before you ever read the label, before you check the ingredients, your brain has already decided, *That looks exciting.* Vibrant packaging signals fun, excitement, reward, and energy. It appeals to emotion before discernment ever has a chance to engage.

As you push your shopping cart down the aisle, low-nutritional products, especially cereal boxes, shout at you: "Buy me!" "Try me!" "I'm delicious!" "It's party time." "Take me home." Marketers understand that if they can capture your attention, they can influence your choice. Therefore, that is the reason the cereal aisle looks like a carnival. It is called visual stimulation. Ultra-processed foods compete fiercely for notice, and in that competition, the loudest packaging usually wins. That is why cereal boxes often look more like toy packaging than food.

By contrast, the healthiest foods in the store tend to sit quietly. Their packaging is simpler. Fewer colors. Less noise. They do not rely on hype because they don't have to. Their value is not in how loudly they announce themselves, but in what they produce once consumed.

With a renewed focus on what we put into our bodies, greater attention has been given to actually seeing what ingredients are in our food. There is more there than most people realize. A recent study found that 60 percent of all foods sold in America have additives such as colors, flavors, preservatives, sweeteners, thickeners, stabilizers, and other chemicals, just to name a few.[10]

These additives do make the food taste good and last longer; however, studies indicate that the highly processed foods negatively affect long-term health. They stimulate, but they do not sustain.

The conclusion is difficult to ignore: the more unhealthy a food is, the more it depends on pizzazz packaging to compete for attention and consumption. However, healthy food can stand confidently without shouting. Its worth is proven not by packaging but by the results it produces over time.

I know what you're thinking: What does food packaging have to do with revival and spiritual growth? It matters more than most might realize.

If we are not careful, it is possible to consume only what is colorful, stimulating, exciting, energetic, and eventful, while neglecting what is healthy for our spiritual advancement. Just as the loudest packaging often hides the poorest nutrition, the most sensational—and dare I say emotional—spiritual experiences do not always produce the deepest transformation. Some believers become spiritual consumers, moving from one place to the next in search of the next encounter, the next atmosphere, or the next "new thing." They are drawn to what excites them, not necessarily to what forms them. Stimulation is not bad at all, but spiritual maturity takes more than this alone.

God desires something much different. God is far more concerned with formation than stimulation. He is focused on the journey, the process of maturity that ultimately has you conforming to the image of Jesus. Formation produces strength, endurance, and residual fruit. The spiritual life was never designed to move in circles. It was designed to move in cycles.

God does not lead His people in circles; He leads them in cycles. However, we can get in the way of His plans as we often do, so let me put it this way: God never *desires* to lead His people in circles;

He *wants* to lead them in cycles. Circles imply stagnation, endless motion with no progress. Circles are like a treadmill, motion, repetition, and activity without advancement. It is the same terrain.

Cycles, however, are intentional, purposeful. Cycles cover territory; they carry movement, direction, and transformation. Cycles advance and take you from one season to the next. Scripture affirms this pattern clearly: *"To everything there is a season, a time for every purpose under heaven"* (Ecclesiastes 3:1 NKJV). God designed life to move through seasons. Movement is normal. Transition is expected. Progress is His intention.

Understanding this changes how we interpret seasons that feel long, difficult, or repetitive.

IT ISN'T THE DEVIL'S FAULT

Whenever we are spiritually stuck and seem to go in circles, we need to reevaluate and ask the tough questions: "Why am I still here in the same place?" "Why is this happening again?" "Why can't I overcome?" "Why is God doing this to me?"

Remaining stuck in one season is not healthy, nor is it His desire. God wants to take us through seasons. His heart is progress, growth, and maturity, not stagnation. At times, prolonged seasons are not the result of spiritual attack but of resisted transformation. We have delayed or avoided the work the Holy Spirit intended to accomplish in that moment.

We cannot miss this next truth. In fact, it will set you free. Each season is designed to serve us and prepare us for the next season that God has for us. However, if we resist the development required—spiritually, emotionally, relationally—we unintentionally delay what God longs to release. The harvest of the next season is postponed, not because God is unwilling, but because He is wise.

This can be discouraging. It can feel confusing. And if we are honest, we often prefer a simpler explanation. So what do we do? We tend to blame the devil.

But sometimes it isn't the devil at all. Sometimes it is our reluctance to change.

Imagine a student who has been in the same grade for years. The teacher is ready. The next classroom is ready. The curriculum for the next level has already been prepared. The problem is not the school system. The problem is that the student has not completed the work required to move forward.

No one blames the principal for holding the student back. No one blames the building. No one blames the calendar. Everyone understands the truth: promotion follows preparation.

God works the same way.

Consider an athlete who dreams of competing at the highest level but refuses the discipline of training. The athlete skips workouts, avoids conditioning, and neglects practice. When competition arrives, the athlete feels unprepared and frustrated. It would be easy to blame the coach. Easy to blame the schedule. And even easier to blame the competition. But the real issue would be the training that never happened. The discipline required to get better never materialized.

The same is true in relationships. Imagine a marriage struggling with communication, but neither spouse is willing to grow, apologize, or learn new patterns. Years can pass while the same arguments repeat themselves. The relationship feels stuck, going in circles like a car race, but the real issue is resistance to growth.

Progress requires participation. In order to grow and to break out of unhealthy patterns, we must change. The sooner we learn that our cooperation and submission to God are key components to spiritual growth, the quicker we will mature.

Consider these statements closely: The Holy Spirit does not keep us in seasons to punish us. He keeps us there to mature us. What feels like delay is often mercy. What feels like stagnation is often preparation. What feels like restriction is often protection.

The question shifts from "Why is the enemy delaying me?" to "What is the Spirit developing in me?"

Every season has a purpose, and every purpose is preparing you for what comes next. The goal of God is not to exhaust you with repetition but to mature you through progression. Circles exhaust. They take us nowhere, but cycles transform.

When God leads in cycles, everything has purpose; nothing is wasted. Every hard season builds endurance. Every hidden season builds roots. Every peaceful season allows us to rest and catch our breath. Every joyful season expands our vision. Every stretching season increases capacity. What feels slow is often sacred. What feels repetitive is often refining.

The invitation of every season is simple: trust and cooperate with the work of the Holy Spirit. When we do this, circles become cycles. And seasons that once felt endless suddenly become stepping stones.

God does not lead His people in circles.

He leads them forward.

5

THE DANGER OF THE MIDDLE

Dawsonville, Georgia, is a car racing city. Some of our most well-known citizens have been involved in the car racing industry on many levels. The most famous member of our city is Bill Elliott, affectionately known to NASCAR fans as "Awesome Bill from Dawsonville." He is one of the most respected and beloved drivers in NASCAR history. He literally put this small Appalachian city on the map when he captured the NASCAR Winston Cup Championship in 1988 and was named NASCAR's Most Popular Driver (a title he would win 16 consecutive times, 1985–2000). He is also the father of Chase Elliott, who won the 2020 NASCAR Cup Series Championship.

When you drive through our town, you will see that many of our streets are named after people who were involved in racing. Some of the businesses have old race cars in front of their establishments. Also, the Georgia Racing Hall of Fame is located in Dawsonville.

During a race, the racers know the place they want to avoid the most, the middle. Why? The middle of the pack is the most dangerous place to be, not because the drivers lack skill, but because the margin for error disappears. Every experienced driver understands this: one small mistake or miscalculation by another driver can have devastating results for those in the middle.

If they stay in the middle too long, they dramatically increase their chances of wrecking, stalling momentum, or losing the race altogether. In the middle, a driver has the least amount of control. It is no longer a place of leading; it is a place of survival. They are in a constant reactionary mode.

Spiritually, many believers have settled into the middle. Not opposed to God, but not fully surrendered to Him either. This portion of the chapter is about the hidden danger of middle-of-the-pack Christianity and God's invitation to wholehearted devotion.

In racing, if you are out front, you have clean air, vision is clear, and you move your car strategically. Your objective is to find the fastest groove and hold the line. Go as fast as you can and keep everyone else behind you. In the midst of a collection of cars, the air becomes dirty, which affects the airflow into the engine, the surroundings are turbulent, and the car can lose its grip, traction, and efficiency. Even engines built to lead become severely limited by congestion in the middle.

However, for the believer, the middle has become a safe place. Here is why. You have options. You are not fully committed, but you are not fully gone either. Furthermore, it releases greater responsibilities to others. And it lets others do the heavy lifting. While the one in the middle can swoop in to enjoy the benefit of the hard work of others.

There is safety in the middle, but there is also danger. The middle is where people, for the most part, stop making serious choices. They are in a cycle of compliance. Comfort is their idol of choice.

We often hear phrases like "Stay balanced," "Tap the brakes," or "Don't go overboard." These words are usually well-intended. And in many areas of life, balance is wise. But spiritually, they can quietly become permission to remain in the middle, which could be hazardous.

Balance is a pseudo-spiritual way of saying, "Stay in the middle. Take care of yourself." In Scripture, God repeatedly called people to wholehearted surrender, not into a life of moderation. Balance demands no courage and neuters the bodacious faith necessary to become counter culture. Balance has boundaries to obedience. It does not mean the middlers disobey God at all times, but there are limits to their "yes." They will obey for only so much, so far, and for so long.

The middle often gives way to convenient obedience. This type of person has fluctuating convictions that are tolerant and inclusive. They do not want to stand out as being extreme or narrow-minded.

In addition, the person in the middle most likely has embraced a brand of Christianity that is entertainment-based. It seeks pleasure and will avoid any commitment that calls for extreme surrender.

The middle is beige and grey, neutral, uncommitted, and dare I see neither hot nor cold, it is lukewarm. It focuses on "fitting in" and, at the end of the day, looks to survive. Here in the middle, everything is negotiated, a give-and-take if you will. Restraint and spiritual comfort are the norm. The outcomes are weighed, and if the cost is too high, then it must not be God's best for them.

I hear the voice of the prophet Elijah echoing in my head as he confronted Israel's indecision head-on: *"How long will you waver between two opinions?"* (1 Kings 18:21 NIV). Then there is the apostle Paul, who demanded his fellow believers to *"Come out from among them and be separate…"* (2 Corinthians 6:17 NIV). Run along the edge, join the others who chose a different path; people including David, Daniel, Noah, John the Baptist, Esther, Elijah, Timothy, Mary, John, Stephen, Deborah, and Ruth.

History rarely records the movements of the pack, but history is normally kind to those who choose to swim upstream; those who choose to leave the bunch to blaze a different trail. Names such as Dietrich Bonhoeffer, Martin Luther King Jr., Abraham Lincoln, Joan of Arc, Winston Churchill, and Mother Teresa are just a few who chose to walk a different path.

If you choose not to walk in the middle of the pack, I promise you this: you will not be alone, but there will not be many. You will find yourself in the company of rare men and women who chose what was best, not what was safest.

Yes, the path is narrow. It is less traveled. But the view and experiences on that narrow path last a lifetime.

Doing life in the middle makes minimal memories. The adventures are coordinated, and a safe landing is always the outcome. And sadly, you are left telling someone else's story, their journey, their tales of adventure and victory. However, the narrow way, the path away from the masses, if you so choose, allows you to leave a legacy that those closest to you will speak of over and over.

SIGNS YOU MAY BE LIVING IN THE MIDDLE

You may be living in the middle if:

- You want God's blessings more than God's transformation
- You avoid obedience that feels costly
- You rarely feel stretched by faith
- You prefer comfort over calling
- You admire bold faith in others but hesitate to live it yourself
- You delay surrender
- You live with spiritual passivity

The enemy is content when believers stay in the middle. Why? Because it is deceptively comfortable. It is powerless and non-influential. One who is in the middle is like a scentless candle—nothing more than a sparkle. These people do not shape history; they get absorbed by it. They do not control the narrative; the narrative controls them. They live a life of complicity—one of the most boring places on earth, very little awe, if any.

Life on the edge of obedience is both adventurous and costly. It requires courage. But it is where God does His deepest work. It is the place where momentum slows, urgency fades, and clarity begins to blur. The middle feels safe because it is familiar, but it is often where purpose quietly bleeds out.

When you are serious about your relationship with God, He will never ask you to be balanced—but He will ask you to be faithful, sometimes uncomfortable, and wholeheartedly surrendered.

Jesus never called anyone to follow Him at a distance. He called them to leave nets, leave boats, leave comfort, and follow fully.

The middle may feel safe, but it is not where transformation happens. It is not where history is shaped. It is not where revival is born. The middle is where momentum slows. The edge is where faith grows. God is not asking you to be reckless, but He is asking you to be fully surrendered.

The question is simple: Will you stay in the middle?

6

THE NEED FOR UNDERSTANDING

We are living in an instant information age. We can know anything about everything with a few clicks. With an internet search or with the assistance of AI, we can overflow our minds with information. Information is good; however, information alone does not produce maturity, nor does it grant kingdom effectiveness. Having understanding is one of the key ingredients to not only surviving in the end times but thriving in the midst of it.

Acting without understanding is risky. It leaves people vulnerable to emotionalism, hurt feelings, and despair, which leads to confusion and wasted time. Thus, it allows the enemy to manipulate us on all levels.

God understands the value and permanence of understanding:

- Proverbs 4:5 (NKJV) – *"Get wisdom! Get understanding!"*
- Proverbs 4:7 (NKJV) – *"Wisdom is the principal thing; therefore get wisdom. And in all your getting, get understanding."*
- Proverbs 2:2-3 (NKJV) – *"...apply your heart to understanding; ...lift up your voice for understanding."*

Understanding is not a spiritual gift automatically given by God. It is not that simple; it is to be intensely pursued by those who long to eat from its fruit.

Here is what I have discovered personally, as well as corporately. A lack of understanding of how God works in our lives can lead us to heightened frustration, disappointment, and shallow living. In the worst cases, it can lead some to have a spiritual collapse altogether.

There are moments in life when what we need most is not more power, strength, more zeal, or even more faith, but understanding. Understanding not only gives meaning to pressure, but it also helps us interpret its purpose. Understanding helps us cope with delay. It explains pain. And most importantly, it keeps us from quitting in seasons when quitting feels reasonable.

In the contemporary version of Christianity that most of us were brought up in, people have adopted the mindset that resistance of any kind means something is wrong. They assume resistance means rejection. Some feel that delay means denial, but this simply is not true. Without understanding, we forfeit divine moments of intimacy and growth.

Your Christian journey does not move in a straight line; it moves in cycles. Each phase has its own tests, trials, temptations, and carries its own demands. When we understand the season we are in, we can endure it, steward it, and even grow stronger because of it.

But when we fail to recognize this revelation of seasons, we often fight and vehemently reject the very process God is using to prepare us for what comes next. God always wants to prepare us for the next phase in our lives.

Scripture tells us that *"the sons of Issachar had understanding of the times, to know what Israel ought to do…"* (1 Chronicles 12:32 NKJV). Their strength was not in their numbers, weapons, or even their courage; it was clarity.

I have made tons of mistakes because I reacted rather than responded to situations. I moved out of emotion or fears. There is a difference between *reacting* to a situation and *responding* to something. Understanding separates reaction from responding. When we have understanding, we can slow down our reaction impulse. Understanding affords the space so we can respond correctly, with wisdom. It allows an individual to navigate complexity without losing focus. It keeps our feet on solid ground.

Understanding allows us to put the pieces together and know that what is happening is normal and manageable; therefore, we live intentionally rather than reactively. Sadly, many people abandon what God is doing simply because they misinterpret the season they are in.

Scripture repeatedly connects understanding with long life and favor. How is this possible? It enables a person to apply truth, reason, and appropriate action steps in the midst of changing seasons. It stabilizes decision-making, as well as our reaction to what we don't quite understand.

Understanding keeps us out of an emotional ditch. We all know what happens when we respond from emotions alone. Dare I say the outcome is rarely good for the long term. Proverb 2:10-11 (NKJV) says, *"When wisdom enters your heart, and knowledge is pleasant to your soul, discretion will preserve you; understanding will keep you."*

Understanding will keep you. The Hebrew word for *keep* means to guard from dangers, watch over, to keep, to preserve, to blockade you in. Wow! The benefits of operating with wisdom and understanding are outstanding. This behooves us to get understanding. It makes us stable and unable to be penetrated by deceit and sin.

Having understanding regarding the seasons of your life keeps situations in perspective. Your mind and heart will be guarded and blockaded by your renewed mind that relies on the peace of the Holy Spirit to govern them.

This is most true when it comes to the changing seasons you will encounter as a believer. Because some in the body of Christ lack understanding regarding the different phases they will walk through, unnecessary casualties occur. With proper understanding, believers will maintain the right posture and keep their priorities in place.

Let me give you some practical advice. When you are walking through a season, go ahead and name it, label it. Then begin to discern it. Ask these three questions:

1. "What is God forming in me right now?"
2. "What is He preparing me for?"
3. "What can I do to maximize this time of waiting?"

Those questions will assist you greatly as you walk through your season. Because once you understand where you are and why you are there, you are far less likely to walk away from where God is taking you.

I want to navigate you through the four seasons or cycles that you and your church will walk through every year. It is like clockwork. These seasons are as dependable as the natural seasons of spring, summer, fall, and winter.

In this book we look at them in the following sequence:

- Stimulation Phase (spring) - 13 weeks
- Sanctification Phase (summer) - 13 weeks
- Shock and Awe Phase (fall) - 13 weeks
- Service Phase (winter) - 13 weeks

As you see, each phase lasts approximately three months. Yes, three months! How do I know that? I lived through it. I have experienced it, and each phase is similar to our natural seasons: spring, summer, fall, and winter. You need to understand this in your spirit—it will help you as you move forward in life.

GOOD NEWS AND BAD NEWS

First, the good news: God will be with you every step of the way. These seasons are for your good and His glory.

Bad news: I have been through this cycle every year for multiple years. That's right, every year. You will walk through this each and every year, too. It's not a one-and-done. It is cyclical.

This book acts as a stabilizer, because you will know the reason for every season.

7

HE WANTS YOUR SHOES

Transitions are part of God's plan. Transitions are the sacred in-between spaces that demand a response from all who want to fulfill the purpose God has for them. However, this is one of the most misunderstood and dangerous phases of a person's walk with the Lord. Why? They mistake the Lord's stillness and silence for rejection. They associate loss of intimacy with the Lord as if He is disappointed in them; therefore, He has withdrawn Himself. These thoughts cannot be further from the truth. Transition is neither a loss nor is it rejection, it is preparation for the next that God has for you.

I want to help you recognize when God is moving you into a new season and how to respond with faith instead of fear.

I get it. Transitions are difficult to interpret and challenging to navigate, especially in sessions of revival. Yet they are unavoidable. Every genuine move of God requires movement, and movement always demands transition. Transitions are a way of life.

For example:

- A newborn transitions into the toddler stage
- A young person leaves home for college
- A career change that demands relocation
- Ministries evolve and assignments shift

Transitions are seldom easy. But they are always purposeful. They push our boundaries and beckon us into unfamiliar waters. They stretch faith and require us to trust Him and His ways. The purpose of God transitioning you is not punishment; it has to do with placement. It is God's way of lifting us from one dimension of usefulness to another.

Transition is not the exception in life—it is the normal pathway to growth. However, if we refuse to transition properly, we can become stagnant and severely limited in our growth opportunities, if not totally off limits.

WHY ARE TRANSITIONS SO DIFFICULT?

For starters, transitions are difficult because we love routines. We love rhythms and familiarity. We wrap our arms around the predictable because we feel safe knowing what is next. When transition is upon us, we get nervous because an old way of living or doing something is ending, and the next is not quite clear yet. The future is undefined and unsettled. We move from what is known to the unknown, which can trigger anxiety.

Transitions are most problematic for people who are used to routines. We are leaving what we understand, but haven't yet arrived at what we will understand. God asks us to trust Him before we see with our natural eyes—and the space between those two can be unsettling.

Think about standing on the last step of a staircase in the dark. You know the floor is coming, but you can't see it. You are unsure how far the floor is. While balancing yourself, you try to find the floor with your other foot. That final step always feels awkward, and you are cautious. Transitions feel exactly like that.

Seasons and transitions allow God to move us from where we have been to where we must go next. For example, caterpillars don't become butterflies instantly. There is a transition—a cocoon season. Transitions feel difficult, not because something is wrong, but because something is changing. And change is the birthplace of growth. It is His way.

ADDED WEIGHT OF GLORY

Each season you go through, and the transition that follows, is a tool that God uses to prepare you physically, emotionally, mentally, and spiritually for the added weight of glory He is placing on you. Transitions are uncomfortable because they stretch us, they challenge our routines, but they are also the doorway to everything new God wants to do.

Every new assignment in your life requires new strength. Before Joseph could rule, he transitioned through pits, prisons, and palace service. Before David sat on a throne, he transitioned through fields, sheep, caves, and deserts. Before Elijah passed his mantle, Elisha had to transition from plowing to following.

I have learned that going from one season to the next, the process and transition shake off what cannot go with me into the next season. For example, I don't wear a winter coat in summer, nor do I wear flip-flops in winter. I have a completely different wardrobe for each season.

Not everything can travel with you to the next season. What is good for one season may not be intended to go into the next season. They simply cannot make the trip with you. Some things, and at times good things, have to be left behind. I remember when God spoke to Moses, *"Take off your sandals, for the place where you are standing is holy ground"* (Exodus 3:5 NIV).

Moses had a choice. He could have decided to keep his shoes on and miss the "next" God had for him. He could have stated, "These shoes got me here, why can't I keep them on? They are part of me." It didn't matter to God that his shoes were meaningful to Moses. He made it clear that "those shoes cannot accompany you as you draw closer to Me."

This leads me to ask the question: "What shoes are you willing to step out of in order to get closer to God?" Everything has to be on the table. At this juncture, we cannot afford to cling to anything. Do not be surprised if He asks for your shoes, for He will ask. God often asks us to release what was right for the last season so we can receive what is right for the next one.

Throughout Scripture, God speaks most clearly during transitions. Why? He loves the next in our lives, and He wants us to get it right.

He spoke to Abraham when he left home. He spoke to Moses in the wilderness. He spoke to Joshua as leadership changed. He spoke to the disciples as Jesus ascended.

During transition, God will speak to you; He will not be absent nor unexpressive. His direction will be clear and requires your highest trust.

In the chapters that follow, you will see the beauty and necessity of transitions.

PART TWO

THE STIMULATION PHASE

8

REVIVAL IS HERE!

Revival assumes something important—prior life.

Revival is not God creating something brand-new. It is God awakening what already belongs to Him. You do not revive what has never lived. You revive what has grown cold.

When revival truly touches the heart, affection is reordered. A renewed love for God rises and begins displacing lesser loves. What once satisfied no longer does. Carnal appetites begin to fade away, not because someone preached against them, but because a superior affection has taken place.

One thing I have consistently noticed in every revived heart is that the old loses its grip. Sin becomes intolerable, not merely because it is forbidden, but because it contradicts love. What once felt acceptable now feels foreign, like it does not belong; it feels invasive. This shift does not happen through self-discipline alone. It comes through repentance, through a heart that turns fully back to God. Revival does not introduce something new; it restores what was abandoned.

MORE THAN DISCONTENTMENT

Being spiritually dissatisfied with our current condition is not enough to bring revival. Frustration does not equal transformation.

Dissatisfaction alone changes nothing. Complaints do not produce transformation. And I would even dare to say that desperation by itself is still not enough.

Do not misunderstand, both dissatisfaction and desperation are necessary. They are important signals, warning lights, but they are not sufficient to bring revival. Something more is required.

Consider a thirsty man in the desert. He may be deeply dissatisfied with his condition. He may even be desperate for water. That desperation creates urgency, but if he does not move toward a source, he still dies, and his desperation was meaningless.

In the same way, spiritual desperation without response is only emotion. It may be sincere. It may be intense. But unless it leads to repentance, obedience, and decisive movement toward God, it produces no change. The first waves of revival begin when our longing produces movement.

Revival is not born from how badly we want God to move; it is born when our longing finally pushes us to pursue Him with no strings attached.

GOD'S SIDE AND OUR SIDE

Revival has two sides: God's side and man's side. While God is always willing to move, we have to cooperate with Him. Revival is not a mechanical sovereign event imposed on unwilling people.

I am convinced our side gets a vote. We choose whether we will draw near or remain distant. We decide whether we will cooperate with the Holy Spirit or resist Him. Yes, we can resist the will and operation of the Holy Spirit, and the Scriptures straightforwardly warn us to not do it (Acts 7:51). When our cooperation is withheld, the work God desires to accomplish is either limited or never realized.

Let me be clear. To many, revival appears to come in an instant. However, revival does not arrive in a single dramatic moment. It is not as though one minute revival is absent and the next minute it suddenly appears. It does not work that way. Revival is rarely spontaneous; it is progressive. There are a lot of small steps along the way.

Revival comes as the result of a series of decisions, often costly ones, that lead a person to the end of themselves. It is the slow crushing of the heart that leaves someone empty with no hope but Jesus. It is here where self-sufficiency dies and where overused excuses collapse. It is from this place that a person seeks God and will not stop until He is found. Revival is born when someone would rather die than not discover again the God who saved their soul.

The believer must eventually come to the end of casual and shallow expressions of faith and begin to cry out, not for experiences, but for the living God Himself. When this happens, God notices. God does not glance briefly and move on; He looks intently. He listens attentively.

Second Chronicles 16:9 (NKJV) says, *"For the eyes of the Lord run to and fro throughout the whole earth, to show Himself strong on behalf of those whose heart is loyal to Him...."*

Notice what God is searching for. Not talent. Not influence. Not gifting. Not visibility. He is searching for devotion, loyalty, and a heart that is fully surrendered to Him.

As we repent and humility moves to the forefront, the craving for attention, recognition, and promotion begins to lose its power. God then responds in mercy and draws near to us. As the distance closes, the flame that once flickered begins to burn again.

FIRST LOVE

Jesus says to the church in Revelation, *"But I have this [one charge to make] against you: that you have left (abandoned) the love that you had at first [you have deserted Me, your first love]"* (Revelation 2:4 AMPC).

Notice what Jesus did *not* say. He did not say they *"lost* their first love," He said they *"left,* abandoned, their first love." A backslidden heart does not misplace its love for God; it walks away from it; they leave it behind. They ignore it.

How does that happen? How can someone who, at one time, was red-hot in love with Jesus come to a place where love has simmered? No one intends for this to happen, but it can and does. It happens slowly, quietly, as affections shift. The eyes of the heart get infatuated with other things, and interest fades. Distractions creep in, and devotion is divided.

The issue is not that backsliders stop believing in God; they stop loving Him the way they once did. Backsliding does not begin with the abandonment of doctrine, discipline, or devotion. It begins when the love cools.

Charles Spurgeon warned: "God will not be content with a divided heart. He must be loved first and best, or not at all."[11] The abandonment of our first love is serious. It damages our relationship with Jesus, weakens our witness, fractures fellowship, and diminishes the life of the Church. However, true revival restores first love.

THE UNBELIEVABLE OPPORTUNITY

Revival gives the Church an extraordinary opportunity. It creates space for Jesus to express Himself to the world without the man-made obstacles we so often place in His way. The barriers, at least temporarily, are set aside. The spirit of religion that seeks to control what God can and cannot do loses its authority. Our religious systems loosen their grip, and the need to manage outcomes is quieted, thus allowing the Founder and Owner of the Church to conduct His business as He sees fit.

When revival comes individually or corporately, it begins the Stimulation Phase of your journey!

9

THE JOURNEY BEGINS

When God's glory came into our building on February 11, 2018, revival came to Christ Fellowship Church in Dawsonville, Georgia. Needless to say, my life changed. My family changed. My whole world was turned upside down. It impacted our church, and it has never been the same. Even to this day, His glory is among us.

Scottish evangelist Duncan Campbell, who led the mid-20th-century Hebrides Revival, said, "When God steps down, revival begins."[12] True revival begins with unparalleled power. Those present at its inception experience what is often the defining encounter of their faith journey.

People feel loved again. Accepted. Valued. An inexpressible joy floods the heart. Tears flow easily and sometimes for no reason at all. Worship matters again and almost feels effortless. Testimonies multiply as people share all that God has and is doing in their lives. The heart feels light, almost weightless. Their relationship with God becomes simple again.

EVERYONE LOVES IT

When a move of God truly comes to a church, the vast majority of people love it. There is a renewed awareness of God that prevails among the people, young and old alike. They are energized, awakened, and fall in love with Jesus the first time or all over again. It is a beautiful sight to behold and even more precious to experience it. The overwhelming sentiment is that people want this "new" thing to last forever; they never want these feelings and experiences to dissipate.

The first phase of a true revival is beautiful and glorious. I call this phase the Stimulation Phase. This initial phase is the honeymoon of revival, the early days when heaven seems to touch everything with color, clarity, and possibility. It is the season when God begins by healing the obvious.

One of the most beautiful manifestations that occurs during this phase is this: *God fixes everything everyone knows is broken.*

This is what makes the early days of the revival so exhilarating and fun. People can't wait to get to the meeting to "see" what God is going to do next. It is in this season that God repairs the broken marriage that everyone knows is in trouble. He meets the prodigal at the altar and welcomes him back home. He saves the sinner who has been on the prayer list for months. He delivers the deacon's drug addict son. This phase is awe-inspiring and thrilling; there is nothing like it. People come into the building with great expectation and sit on the edge of their seats waiting to see what is next.

Again, in this phase, God touches, delivers, heals, and restores what "everyone" already knows is beyond human effort.

In this phase, people are eyewitnesses to His glory. They hear the stories as individuals stand up and testify of God's love and delivering power. They see hardened men cry, and young people come out of darkness. Across the board, no one wants this revival to end.

In addition, the worship becomes more than something to endure; it is an interaction with God. People feel as if He is present and singing directly to Him—and He is enjoying every sound and word.

Plus, differences among church members are minimized, and unity is the result. Nothing matters but Him and His purposes.

God goes to work, and everyone knows heaven has come to earth. The hearts of the people have been touched, and they feel more alive than they ever have. Their vision is unclouded, their hearing is clearer. But ultimately, in the beginning climate of revival, the overwhelming cry from the hearts of those involved is the following prayer: "How close can I get to you, God, on this side of eternity? That is where I want to be. Take me there!"

That is the cry of the Stimulation Phase.

It is beautiful.

And it is only the beginning.

10

I WATCHED A MAN DIE!

Moments matter. Few moments have stayed with me like the instant Zach turned the corner and cautiously approached the baptismal tank. He was visibly nervous; I could see it in his posture, in the hesitation of each step. He looked unsettled, almost undone. It was week 40 of the North Georgia Revival, and I had a front-row seat to one of the most powerful moves of the Spirit I have ever witnessed, a holy collision between destruction and a new beginning.

Zach stepped into the water carrying an enormous weight on his shoulders. His future felt suspended in that moment. He stood on the edge of a decision that would change the course of his life.

The North Georgia Revival has become a place where people from around the world come to be immersed and encounter God in the water. They come ready to bury the past. They are tired of torment and trauma; they step into the water to lay down the old life and rise into something new with God.

It has become our custom, once someone enters the water, to ask four simple questions:

What is your name?

Where are you from?

Why are you in the water?

And finally, do you want to hold your nose?

After settling into the water, he answered the first two questions.

"My name is Zack. I'm from Kennesaw, Georgia."

Then came the third question, the one that matters most.

"Why are you in the water?"

He said, "I am here for my marriage…something I didn't think I would say after only two years in. My wife and I are on different walks with the Lord right now. And I have given everything over to Him. The enemy has come in trying to cause a divide. I know what God has prophesied over our family. I have kinda just worn thin a little bit, and I need power and the refreshing fire of the Holy Spirit in my life so I can take it back to my home. And see my wife, I miss my wife. I miss my wife being next to me, pursuing the Lord. I just didn't think I would be here two years into our marriage. But the enemy is not going to have her. It is personal, and he [the devil] can go back to hell; he is not going to have her. I am believing Jesus."

THEN IT HAPPENED

Zach was baptized in the "fire water" at the North Georgia Revival. A place we had seen bodies healed, people delivered, and prodigals come home.

I watched a man die right there in the water. He did not stop breathing, but he might as well have. If I have ever seen God strike a man, it was this man. God knocked him out, and before my eyes, Zack looked like he was dead, but at the same time, while completely immobile, looked to be at perfect peace.

In these few but precious moments, God was performing surgery on Zach's heart. Everything changed in a moment. When he stood up, Zach was a totally new man; everything shifted. He was empowered with power and purpose. His marriage was being healed before he emerged from the water.

He went home that night, and nothing appeared to be changed. They were still not on talking terms. The following Monday, after buying groceries together, Zach and Melissa began to put the groceries away. However, he heard gospel music playing through the speaker connected to their TV. He thought that was weird and walked over to see what was happening. The television was off, but music was coming through the speaker. Then the Holy Spirit spoke to him, "I have angels in your house, and they are changing the atmosphere." From that moment, things shifted in their relationship; each day their marriage improved, better and better. Then one afternoon, she said, "I want to go to the revival."

HER TURN

Four weeks after Zach's baptism, on December 3, Zach returned to the water. However, he did not come alone. Walking through the water in front of him was his wife, Melissa.

Here is what she said when asked, "Why are you in the water?"

Melissa: "I should have been here a long time ago. The devil has completely stolen my joy to the point where I do not want to go to church anymore. It has caused me to have bitterness toward my husband. I want my own testimony—I don't want to live under his anymore, I want my own. And I want to be on fire. I want to do life with my husband like God has taught us to do. I want it to start tonight."

The same power that met her husband in the water four weeks earlier met her as well. In a moment, the Lord turned her world right-side up, healing what had been broken, softening what had grown hard, and restoring the joy she had longed to feel again. In an instant, the heaviness lifted. God met her in the place she needed Him most.

After the Lord ministered to them both in the water, I stepped forward, and I asked them if they would like to renew their wedding vows to one another. Without hesitation, they said yes. So, in the middle of the baptismal tank, on an international television broadcast, with their heads bowed and their foreheads gently touching, they renewed their promises, vowing once again to love, honor, and serve one another.

That night, they stepped into the water carrying pain, questions, and uncertainty. They stepped out carrying hope, restoration, and a fresh beginning. They did not just leave the water wet; they left changed, having encountered the living God together.

RESTORATION POWER WORKED!

Nine months later, a baby boy was born. The following is a post from Zack's Facebook page. A picture is posted of him holding and kissing his newborn son in a wheat field. What follows is the message of reflection that Zack wrote to his son:

> *You are the product of Jesus's restoring power, born from true revival. Your name "Dawson" comes from Dawsonville, Georgia, where at a revival, Jesus met your mommy and me and healed our marriage. "Graham" is after Billy Graham, a mighty evangelist/servant of the Lord whom God used to bring millions to Jesus.*
>
> *Daddy and mommy have been praying over you since the day we found out you were on the way, and have known since day one that the Lord has something special in store for you.*
>
> *I did not realize until today how prophetic this picture is, standing in a field "that is ready for harvest." Dawson, I believe this is a prophetic glimpse of what the Lord will do through you. Jesus said, "The harvest is ready," and just as you are being carried now in the middle of a field ready for harvest by your earthly daddy, the Lord (Your heavenly Daddy) will be carrying you through a WORLD ready for harvest and will bring millions of people to Jesus through you. Keep your eyes on Jesus, son. He will never fail you, He will never leave you, and you cannot even begin to fathom the love and plans your heavenly Father has for you."*

One moment, one baptism, one encounter, one life changed, and now the world will feel its impact.

This kind of encounter happens frequently in the Stimulation Phase of revival—and is why everyone is excited in the beginning of a move of God.

PART THREE

THE SANCTIFICATION PHASE

THE MOST MISUNDERSTOOD PHASE

11

THEY PRAYED FOR REVIVAL—THEN WALKED AWAY

When revival manifested in our church, within eight months, nearly *200 people left the church.*

I didn't understand why so many people left and exited the revival. To be honest, I was brokenhearted. These were not casual attenders. Many of them had fasted and prayed beside me for revival and were conduits of God's miracle-working power as the Lord healed the very ones they immersed in the water. Yet in the middle of the move of God, they walked away.

I wrestled deeply with the question: Why do people leave in the middle of revival?

The words of pastor and missionary J. Edwin Orr helped prepare the way for me to understand what was happening: "Every revival in history has been birthed out of holiness and maintained through holiness."[13]

For revival to be a reality, there are many contributing factors. However, for it to be sustained and intensified, sanctification is part of the equation. It has always been that way.

And sanctification is where many people turn back.

GOD NEVER WASTES A SEASON

The Lord never wastes a season.

He leads us into different seasons not to harm us, but to reveal what is in our hearts. His agenda is clear: to expose what is hidden. Plus, to show us what we can truly handle regarding the work and weight of God.

Before Israel entered the Promised Land, after 40 years in the wilderness, God explained to Joshua why they had endured the desert:

> *And you shall remember that the Lord your God led you all the way these forty years in the wilderness, to humble you and test you, to know what was in your heart, whether you would keep His commandments or not. So He humbled you, allowed you to hunger, and fed you with manna which you did not know nor did your fathers know, that He might make you know that man shall not live by bread alone; but man lives by every word that proceeds from the mouth of the Lord* (Deuteronomy 8:2-3 NKJV).

This passage gives us some incredible insight into why God takes us through different seasons—especially the sanctification season. Notice the people were in a dry place, the desert. The following are a few key phrases from Deuteronomy 8:2-3 that reveal what God wants to do during seasons of preparation:

- Humble you (verse 2)
- Test you
- See what is in your heart
- Know if you would obey Him when your future is uncertain
- Humble you (verse 3)
- Allow you to hunger, give you just enough
- Teach complete dependence on Him

Wow! This is remarkable. God revealed with great detail what He wanted to accomplish in the heart of Israel. Humble. Test. To know what was in their heart and to see if they would trust Him.

Charles Finney was a minister and Second Great Awakening leader in the United States in the early 19th century. He had an interesting take on the sanctification process: "The process of sanctification is God's method of bringing His children to maturity; it is heaven's education system on earth."[14] This is a beautiful description of how God prepares His children for life and ministry. Finney understood sanctification as one of the primary tools God uses to mature and educate His people.

Maturity proves capacity. When a person matures, they demonstrate that they can handle greater responsibility. Sanctification is one of the ways God prepares us to carry what He desires to entrust to us.

Sanctification also has another purpose—it locates us.

Through the sanctifying work of the Holy Spirit, God reveals our true level of spiritual maturity and dependence on Him. Sanctification removes illusion and replaces it with crystal-clear clarity. It shows us not where we imagine ourselves to be, but where we actually are.

Have you ever stood in a large shopping mall or amusement park and searched for your location on one of the information maps? The entire layout of the park is displayed before you, but what matters most is the small dot or symbol that reads: YOU ARE HERE.

When you discover where you are, the whole picture can come into focus. It is a stabilizing beginning point. Sanctification places a mark on our spiritual lives. It becomes God's way of saying, "This is where you are."

God does not do this to discourage us but to help us. He loves us enough to reveal our true condition so He can lead us forward into greater usefulness. He takes the time necessary to show us where we are so we can move toward where He wants us to be.

We must be careful not to rebel or walk away from the process. When we resist sanctification, we limit our ability to carry greater glory. But when we acknowledge what God is doing and submit ourselves to His work, even if we have resisted in the past, we can repent and continue the journey. God is always willing to resume the work when our hearts return to Him.

GOD IS PREPARING—NOT CONDEMNING

It is important to understand the heart of the Father in the sanctification process.

Often, because of the emotional swings that accompany exposure and correction, and because of the revelation of the brokenness within us, we may feel that God is judging us or disqualifying us. But that is not what He is doing.

God does not expose in order to condemn us. He exposes in order to cleanse. This is a fundamental truth in understanding this and other seasons that may not make sense to us. He reveals to prepare the vessels (us) He desires to use.

Leonard Ravenhill, British evangelist and revivalist preacher, helps us understand this clearly: "God cannot fill what He has not cleansed."[15] Sanctification is not rejection. It is preparation. God is not trying to disqualify us; He is showing us remarkable love because He is qualifying us.

THE EMOTIONS OF REFINING

I have to be honest, every time I go through this process, there is a swirl of emotions within me. I question things. I question His timing, His intentions. At times, I doubt. I wonder. I feel fearful and hopeful at the same time.

And if I am truthful, I often want the process to be over as quickly as possible.

Refining is not comfortable.

Sometimes I don't like what I see when the purifying fire of God is allowed to burn within me. I am often shocked at the dross that surfaces. There are times when I believed I had already conquered a particular issue, only to see it raise its ugly head again.

Influential English Baptist preacher Charles Spurgeon described this experience with piercing honesty: "The nearer a man lives to God, the more intensely has he to mourn over his own evil heart."[16] This revelation is not meant to shame us. It is meant to show us what still needs to be cleansed and uprooted. Lovingly, God reveals so He can heal. He exposes so He can restore.

HOW WE LEAVE THE SEASON

The sanctification process has a beginning and an end. But how we emerge from the season is not automatic. In many ways, we determine how we come out of the season of testing and revealing.

Some emerge bitter, while others emerge discouraged, and sadly, some choose to walk away.

But those who submit and endure during this season emerge stronger, purer, and more prepared for greater usefulness.

SEPARATION PRECEDES POWER

One of the goals of sanctification is separation, a departure from the natural impulses that keep us limited in our effectiveness for the kingdom of God. Duncan Campbell summarized this truth with striking clarity: "Power follows separation."[17]

Vance Havner, American Southern Baptist minister, expressed the same reality from another angle: "Sanctification is the highway on which the fire of revival travels."[18]

The following are some truths I discovered regarding revival:

- Revival does not deepen without sanctification.
- Power does not increase without purification.
- Glory does not rest on what has not been prepared to carry it.

12

AVOID THE EXIT

Every year, millions of people sign up for gym memberships. Recent industry reports estimate that more than 60 million Americans hold gym memberships, but only 44-50 percent of those members use the gym at least twice a week.[19]

Members walk in full of energy. New clothes. New goals. New motivation. They are all in. They are posting pictures of themselves on machines, attending a cycling class, and discussing the small changes in their bodies that working out has caused.

For a moment, everything feels different and looks different, but within a few months, most of them are gone. Absent. Not because the gym failed them, but because the process started working.

Everyone tried to warn them about what was coming, but they wouldn't listen. They didn't calculate for the ongoing soreness they would feel throughout their body. Nor the discipline required for maintaining weight loss and muscle gain. Nor did they factor in the time necessary to get stronger.

This is exactly what happens to many believers. They come to church and have a genuine encounter with God, but over time, the emotions subside, and the transformational process begins.

So the reality is: Stimulation signs you up. Sanctification changes your habits.

I spend a large portion of this book on the season of sanctification. Why? This is the season God moves from visiting you to meticulously working on you. This is the area of greatest misunderstanding, and the result is a consequential number of casualties.

Many believers become discouraged during this season and quietly walk away from the Lord and from His Church. They feel abandoned. They assume they must have done something wrong to deserve what feels like distance from God. When people enter this season without understanding it, they often interpret God's work as God's absence. But what feels like abandonment is often preparation.

Winter is marked by cold, quiet, and reduced momentum. There are unanswered prayers, spiritual fatigue, pruning, silence, clouds, and at times a deep sense of isolation. The vibrant growth of earlier seasons seems to disappear, and life feels slower and less visible.

This is why the season is so easily misinterpreted.

Because of what you feel during this time, it can seem as if the devil has been given free rein in your life. You may feel forgotten. You may feel forsaken. You may feel orphaned. You may feel as if God has withdrawn His nearness.

But the truth is exactly the opposite. What feels like abandonment is actually oversight.

God is carefully watching over your spiritual development. Even when you feel alone, you are not alone. Even when God seems silent, He is still present. Even when progress feels invisible, growth is still taking place. I know it is hard to accept, but actually feeling this is proof that God's intention for this season is underway. Winter is not the absence of God. Winter is the work of God. Call me crazy if you would like, but sanctification, this winter season, is His gift to us.

Let's talk about it like Jesus did. He used the word *pruning* to describe His work in our lives during this phase of our development. Jesus said, "*...every branch that bears fruit He prunes, that it may bear more fruit*" (John 15:2 NKJV). Pruning is one of the clearest pictures of sanctification in all of Scripture.

When pruning begins, a healthy plant does not interpret the cuts as rejection. Obviously, the plant senses a disturbance; however, it responds instinctively to what is happening, for it realizes pruning is the removal of what limits growth and is getting intentionally positioned for greater fruit. The tree shifts into what botanists call compartmentalization.

When a branch is removed, the tree forms a protective barrier around the wound and isolates the damaged tissue so decay cannot spread. The injury is contained so the rest of the tree remains healthy. This is why proper pruning strengthens a tree rather than weakens it.

Something remarkable also happens inside the tree.

Before pruning, the tree's resources are spread across a large number of branches and leaves. After pruning, the tree suddenly has less surface area to support. The same life-giving resources now flow into fewer branches. And the tree's nourishment becomes concentrated. Thus, allowing the remaining branches to receive richer support. Therefore, growth becomes stronger and more dynamic. Even the root system responds by developing greater stability and depth.

The result? The tree becomes more efficient, not less. Stronger, not weaker. Healthier, not damaged.

In the same way, when God prunes our lives, He does so carefully, with the skill of a master botanist. He knows what needs to be cut and when to cut it. He is not removing value, He is revealing value. And one great truth we must embrace: pruning is evidence that the Keeper of the vineyard sees potential worth developing. Pruning is actually an act of love and approval, not rejection.

God prunes what He intends to use.

RESIST THE EMERGENCY EXIT TEMPTATION

You have seen emergency exit doors. On the door are the words: "Emergency Exit — Alarm Will Sound If Used." I accidentally opened one, and the experience was humiliating. When the deafening alarm went off, every head in the restaurant turned and looked at me in great disgust. I felt completely naked, left with nothing but embarrassment. I learned the hard way that these doors need to be avoided and are only meant for a quick exit if a crisis exists. Not convenience.

Yet during the winter season, the devil always makes sure an exit door is nearby. It's human nature that when things become difficult, the temptation to leave becomes strong. Leave the church. Don't trust anyone. Pull back from prayer. Step away from ministry. Reduce your commitment. Protect yourself. Take a break.

One of the greatest dangers of the winter season is escapism, the temptation to flee the very season designed to mature you. When growth becomes uncomfortable, the flesh looks for relief. It is a natural response. But God is not trying to give you relief; He is trying to form you into who He designed you to be.

Winter tempts you to measure God by what you cannot feel and what you cannot see. It whispers that God no longer cares. It suggests that your days of favor are over. It tries to convince you that delay is denial. It tells you the cold means something has gone wrong. Each one of these thoughts is a lie straight from the devil's mouth.

I need to say this again, winter is not evidence that God has stopped working. In fact, the opposite is true; winter is evidence that God is deeply involved in your life and working on you because He cares.

Each time I enter a "winter season," I discover God is accomplishing some of His most necessary work in my heart. Yes, it can be painful. Yes, it can feel lonely. Yes, it can feel slow. But this is where roots deepen. This is where character is tested and formed. It is here where endurance grows and our capacity is enlarged.

Hebrews reminds us: *"You have need of endurance, so that after you have done the will of God, you may receive the promise"* (Hebrews 10:36 NKJV).

Do not reach for the emergency exit when the process becomes uncomfortable. I know the temptation is there, and it is real. We all think about it, but we have to hold on, anchor ourselves, even when we don't understand what is happening in or around us.

Remain steady when unanswered questions swirl about in your head. Let the words of the apostle Paul help you: *"But none of these things move me; nor do I count my life dear to myself, so that I may finish my race with joy"* (Acts 20:24 NKJV).

It is not easy to remain unmoved when the ground beneath is shaking and everything around you seems to be shifting. I admit that freely. It is far easier to say these words than to live them.

But one truth remains constant: God is faithful to His seasons. And He never wastes the cold.

13

THE WATER SCARES ME

Americans are afraid of a lot of things.

According to national surveys, our biggest fears include corrupt government officials, serious illness, economic collapse, cybercrime, and loved ones dying.[20] In other words, we fear losing control, losing safety, and losing the future we thought we could predict.

But there's another fear that rarely makes the national list, yet quietly affects millions of people.

Water.

Fear of water and drowning is one of the most common phobias in the world. Psychologists even gave it a name: aquaphobia. Millions of people avoid pools, lakes, oceans, and even bathtubs because of it. Ironically, humans are surrounded by water; we drink it, bathe in it, and vacation next to it, but many people want absolutely nothing to do with being in it.

It's amazing how comfortable some are standing near the water, as long as they don't have to step into it. What is interesting is that the earth is two-thirds water; it is everywhere.

And spiritually speaking, we're not much different. This chapter is about the fear of going deeper with God. Many believers love the shoreline of faith but hesitate at the thought of surrender. We want God close enough to bless us, but not deep enough to change us. Yet every move of God invites His people further into the river.

Which brings me to a moment from the North Georgia Revival I will never forget.

On week 372, a sweet, normal-looking 76-year-old lady stood trembling in the baptismal water, surrounded by a friend and our baptism team.

The next day, she sent us this message:

> *Hello, I'm Barbara. My testimony might seem small to some, but what God has brought me through is significant to me.*
>
> *I could not enjoy swimming with my kids during the summer due to my fear of water. At 76 years old, I have lived with this fear all my life.*
>
> *My husband's drowning on June 2nd, 1974, worsened my fear and anxiety. However, on week 330 of the North Georgia Revival, June 2nd, 2024 (the anniversary of my husband's passing), I entered the baptismal pool and the Lord healed me of all my water-related fears and anxiety!*

Then she added, "My daughter has booked a cruise for February 2025, and I'm going!"

Guess what?

She went!

This dear woman had a three-second encounter with the Lord in the baptismal water and was completely set free from a fear she had carried for more than seven decades. In a moment, what years of anxiety had built were dismantled by the presence and fire of God. Now she is experiencing things she had avoided, misunderstood, and feared. The water that once represented danger now represents freedom and new adventures. The place she once resisted has become a place of joy. Her story reveals a spiritual truth: the place we fear most is often the place God invites us to encounter Him most deeply.

This brings us to one of the most profound invitations in Scripture. It has to do with water as well.

In Ezekiel 47, the prophet sees a river flowing from the temple of God:

> *Then he brought me back to the door of the temple; and there was water, flowing from under the threshold of the temple toward the east, for the front of the temple faced east; the water was flowing from under the right side of the temple, south of the altar.*
>
> *He brought me out by way of the north gate, and led me around on the outside to the outer gateway that faces east; and there was water, running out on the right side.*
>
> *And when the man went out to the east with the line in his hand, he measured one thousand cubits, and he brought me through the waters; the water came **up to my ankles.***
>
> *Again he measured one thousand and brought me through the waters; the water came **up to my knees**. Again he measured one thousand and brought me through; the water came **up to my waist**.*
>
> *Again he measured one thousand, and it was a river that I could not cross; for the water was too deep, **water in which one must swim**, a river that could not be crossed* (Ezekiel 37:1-5 NKJV).

As you read the text, you will notice that the angel leads him forward and the depth of the water changes in stages:

Ankle deep = newness

Knee deep = adventure and dependence

Waste deep = vulnerability and trust

Waters to swim in = surrender and abandonment

The river did not change direction. The river did not lose power. The river did not stop flowing. The only thing that changed was how far Ezekiel was willing to go. At every stage, he could have stopped. Ankle-deep is new but safe. Knee-deep is more challenging, requires dependence, but is manageable. Waist-deep still allows some control, but more vulnerability and trust is necessary. And swimming requires surrender.

I am convinced it is the Lord's aim to get us out of the shallow end of the river into the deep end. Everything is predictable in the ankle, knee, and waist-deep water. It is comfortable. But God has not saved us to be comfortable. And this is the invitation of sanctification.

The Holy Spirit is preparing our lives to swim in deeper waters. God's purifying fire is not meant to drive us away from the river. It is meant to prepare us to go further into it.

Sanctification prepares you to swim in all God has for you.

Indicators you are standing in the shallow waters:

- You love spiritual experiences but resist spiritual change.
- You want God's comfort more than God's correction.
- You avoid moments of surrender if it is too costly.
- You stay where things are predictable and controllable.
- You hesitate and make excuses each time God invites you to leave the shore.

Here is the stark reality. You and I get to choose how far out we want to go. You can choose whether to stay in the shallows or move toward surrender.

In the natural it is difficult to swim effectively and for any length of time if you are carrying excess weight. The same is true when God asks us to go deeper and to swim in His river. You cannot swim while clinging to debris. You cannot swim while carrying weights. You cannot swim while holding on to what God is asking you to release.

What keeps you in the shallow water? The following are a few reasons that may be keeping you from being totally surrendered:

- Unforgiveness
- Hidden sin
- Bitterness
- Lack of trust
- Neglectful of prayer and Bible study
- Fear of the unknown
- Comfort zones
- Swimming with others who refuse to venture out

Barbara was afraid of water for 76 years; however, one step changed everything.

The river is right in front of you. What will you do? You get to determine how far you will go. What will be your next move?

Step in and swim—it will change everything.

14

THE GREAT REVEAL

Not long ago, the world became obsessed with gender reveal parties—announcing whether the baby will be a boy or girl.

What once was a simple and private matter has now evolved into smoke cannons, fireworks, drones, confetti explosions, flyovers, cakes filled with colored icing, and enough pyrotechnics to rival a small Fourth of July celebration.

And people are spending real money on it.

Event planners estimate the average gender reveal now costs between $300 and $2,000, with elaborate reveals climbing into the tens of thousands of dollars. Social media has fueled the phenomenon. What used to be private news has become a public spectacle. Families want the moment to be unforgettable, shareable, and dramatic.

I have been to a few of these reveal parties, and they can get intense. People dress for the occasion; some show up in pink, others in blue, confidently trying to guess the baby's gender. It almost felt like a friendly competition. The anticipation builds, the suspense grows, and if you're not careful, you can get completely caught up in the excitement. Everything leads to one defining moment, the reveal.

Even with well-thought-out reveals, sometimes things do not go according to plan.

One family planned a reveal using colored smoke inside their home. Within minutes, the smoke alarm blared, the house filled with haze, guests evacuated, and firefighters arrived to make sure the house wasn't burning down. The reveal worked. But the moment was chaotic.

One of the most sobering examples made international headlines. In 2020, a gender-reveal photo shoot in California used a smoke-generating, pyrotechnic device that ignited dry grass and started the El Dorado wildfire. The blaze burned more than 22,000 acres, destroyed homes, forced evacuations, cost over $42 million to fight, and tragically claimed the life of a firefighter.

Just a few years earlier, another gender-reveal stunt in Arizona sparked a wildfire that burned nearly 47,000 acres and caused millions in damage. What began as a joyful announcement became a national disaster.

Gender reveal parties reveal what is hidden; it is the moment when the unknown becomes known. Reveals are powerful because they remove the mystery.

HURRICANES IN THE CHURCH

When a hurricane approaches the coastline, government officials urge residents to evacuate immediately. They understand the danger that is coming. While most people think the greatest threat in a hurricane is the wind, meteorologists consistently warn that the real killer is something else entirely—storm surge.

A storm surge is the massive wall of water that a hurricane pushes inland. It is violent and uncontrollable. Entire neighborhoods can disappear beneath it. Harbors overflow, and streets become rivers. Buildings fill with water as the surge disrupts and displaces nearly everything in its path. Nothing is the same afterward.

But there is another phenomenon, less known and even more unsettling. I remember watching the news coverage as the Gulf Coast prepared for a major hurricane. Meteorologists tracked the storm hour by hour, warning of catastrophic flooding. Everyone expected the water to rise, and it did.

Then something unexpected happened. The blowout tide.

When a hurricane pushes water inland, the surge is obvious. But as the storm rotates and winds begin blowing offshore, the opposite effect can occur. Meteorologists call this a negative storm surge or blowout tide. The same storm that pushed water onto the shore begins pulling it away.

The water that once covered everything now recedes in dramatic fashion. The harbor is now empty, and majestic boats and yachts sit helplessly on the sand. The docks, signs of stability, hang mangled and distorted. The seabed that was covered by water now becomes visible, and everything once hidden is suddenly exposed.

As the water pulls back, you see all types of debris. Broken glass. Beer cans. Discarded tires. Rusted anchors. Broken pilings. Wreckage of all sorts, and even abandoned vehicles, become visible. Things are revealed that no one knew were there.

The storm did not create the mess.

The storm revealed it.

And what is most important to understand is this: the same storm is responsible for both events. It is not two different weather events. The same wind force that pushed water in now pulls the water away from the coastline. The force never stopped; the direction simply changed.

So what do baby gender announcements and blowout tides have in common? Both reveal what is under the surface. Gender reveal parties reveal what is hidden—the unknown becomes known. Reveals are powerful because they remove the mystery. And blowout tides reveal what is buried deeply.

This is sanctification. This is exactly what happens in revival.

In the Stimulation Phase, the Spirit floods the church. His presence rushes in, and the entire atmosphere shifts. Joy rises. Hunger awakens. Prayer increases. Worship intensifies. Love is easy to give and receive. People are open and responsive to the Spirit's promptings. Everything is swallowed up in His goodness. It feels like the tide has come in and will never leave. It feels like a new normal. But then the winds shift.

The same Spirit who flooded the shoreline begins to pull back the water. The wind is still blowing, but in a different direction.

And suddenly, what was hidden beneath the surface is exposed. This is the reveal no one puts on Instagram. This is the reveal no one wants to be public. This is the Great Reveal! The Great Reveal is the moment when the Holy Spirit exposes what celebration not knowingly concealed, including:

- Old unhealthy attitudes
- Hidden pride
- Unconfessed sin
- Broken relationships
- Unhealed wounds
- Compromise we learned to live with

Sanctification feels confusing because the water seems to be leaving just when we thought revival was arriving. This is awkward and unsettling. But heaven understands exactly what is happening. God is not abandoning the coast. He is exposing the debris. He is not removing His presence. He is revealing what His presence uncovered.

THE BLOWOUT TIDE IS MERCY

The blowout tide does not feel like mercy at all; in all honesty, it feels like unmerciful judgment. Everything looks barren, ugly, and even dangerous. It looks empty. I know it is hard to wrap our minds around this, but His mercy is in the midst of it. Because what remains hidden cannot be healed. What lies beneath the surface cannot be removed, nor can it be redeemed. Because God loves us and wants us to encounter more, the revealing and cleansing are necessary.

The enemy will tell you God is angry and abandoning you due to the debris, but that is not true. This season is not evidence that revival is ending. It is evidence that revival is deepening. God is preparing us to carry greater glory.

The Stimulation Phase is the excitement phase when God fixes everything everyone already knows is broken. This is the season when the focus shifts.

But here it is. You may want to make sure you are sitting down before you read it: In the Sanctification Phase, *God exposes, addresses, and fixes things that nobody else knows are broken.* Issues, challenges, and behaviors beneath the surface that no one knows about, that are hidden, tucked away, and in some instances, we don't even know are there.

God puts holy pressure on these areas. Our hearts are laid bare before Him, and He goes after specific areas of compromise. Often these areas have been part of our lives for so long that we barely notice them. But He does. To us, they are not a big deal, but to Him they matter, it is debris and garbage that must be removed. And with laser-like focus, He is coming to help you defeat each one.

The Lord highlights cracks and fractures in our hearts. Things that will impede our capacity, usability, and growth.

But let me be clear—His purpose is not condemnation, it is preparation.

GOD KNOWS WHEN TO EXPOSE

Many people wonder why God waits until revival has begun before exposing what lies beneath. I believe the answer is simple. He draws us close. He reveals His unmatched love and power. He proves His beauty and trustworthiness first. Then He says, "I want to do more in you and through you—but first I must work on your heart." He waits for the perfect moment.

As Solomon wrote: *"He has made everything beautiful in its time"* (Ecclesiastes 3:11 NKJV).

Sanctification is never random. God exposes at the right time. Not too early. Not too late. Exactly when the heart is ready. As *My Utmost for His Highest* author Oswald Chambers noted, "Sanctification is not something we do; it is what God does in us when He gets us to the place where He can."[21]

DON'T LEAVE TOO SOON

One of the greatest dangers of this phase is leaving too soon. I have witnessed people walking away from the Church and the Lord during this time. Why? They didn't understand the Lord's ways, what He was doing. The result? People remain in their current state of spiritual development and usability. And sadly, this is where revivals often lose steam and weaken. This is where misunderstanding produces casualties.

We have to stay until God finishes His work.

Nature teaches the same lesson. A butterfly must complete its time in the cocoon. If the process is interrupted, the butterfly emerges weak and unable to fly. The cocoon is not the destination. The cocoon is the place where butterflies are made, perfected, and prepared to fly.

Sanctification works the same way. Leaving early aborts growth. Avoiding the process delays maturity and deprives us of the opportunity to carry more of His weight.

GOD IS TRANSITIONING THE REVIVAL

In order for the revival to continue and thrive, we must understand the work and intent of the Holy Spirit during this phase. What we often interpret as defeat and decline is more accurately called divine surgery.

He begins the arduous process of the circumcision of the heart. The Spirit is not angry; He is delighted to work on us. Even though we may feel distant and cold, the revival is not over; no, it is preparing to get stronger. The Holy Spirit's power is not leaving; He is revealing.

As Leonard Ravenhill said, "The Holy Spirit does not come to make us happy, He comes to make us holy." He added, "The greatest miracle that God can do today is to take an unholy man out of an un-holy world, make that man holy, and put him back into that world and keep him holy in it."[22]

Sanctification does not mean revival is ending, no, far from it. It means revival is transitioning. God is preparing His people for more, much more. More depth! More authority! More purity! More glory!

The Stimulation Phase awakens hearts. The Sanctification Phase prepares hearts. And when the cleansing is complete—the tide comes back stronger than before.

15

THE WILDERNESS IS NOT THE DESTINATION

The distance from Egypt to Canaan was never the real obstacle.

God heard the groaning of the Israelites in their slavery and sent Moses to Pharaoh. The divine plan was beautifully simple: rescue them from captivity and settle them in a land of their own, a land flowing with milk and honey.

Geographically speaking, the journey was not long. Scholars estimate the distance from the Nile Delta region to the southern border of Canaan at roughly 175-250 miles, depending on the route taken.[23] In other words, the Promised Land was not across an ocean. It was not on another continent. It was just beyond the horizon.

To put this distance in perspective, a person walking at an average pace of two miles per hour could cover that distance in roughly two to three weeks of steady travel.[24] Even accounting for the massive number of people, animals, and supplies involved, many scholars suggest the journey could have reasonably taken several weeks to a few months.

THAT'S A LOT OF PEOPLE

It was not a small road trip. Scripture tells us that about 600,000 men on foot, besides women and children, left Egypt with Moses (Exodus 12:37). When women and children are included, most scholars estimate the population at two to three million people.[25] Imagine the scale: families, elderly grandparents, newborn babies, livestock, carts, tents, food, and the spoils of Egypt, all moving together across the desert. Researchers estimate that each person would need approximately three pounds of food each day.[26] This means the people would consume six million pounds of food every 24 hours. That is 3,000 tons of groceries! Whoa! That's a lot!

And this does not include their drinking water, nor food and water for their livestock. Exodus 12:38 (NKJV) says, *"A mixed multitude went up with them also, and flocks and herds, a great deal of livestock."* And as we all know—animals eat a lot.

So it would be impossible to make the journey in just a few days; it took much longer. However, even with this enormous company, the journey could have been completed in a matter of months.

But things did not go according to plan.

Scripture makes it clear that God intended to lead His people directly into the Promised Land. The 40 years of circling the desert were not part of His original plan. The tragedy of the wilderness journey was multifaceted.

Ultimately, the people of God did not understand the ways of God and resisted His plans. The celebration of freedom, the stimulation of a new life was short-lived. It was great in the beginning; everyone was excited and looking forward to the days to come. A new land, a new home, a new purpose, but something happened that changed everything. Israel grew impatient. They became fearful, and trust became an issue. The more their emotions got involved, the more distracted and resistant they became.

They questioned Moses. They questioned those closest to Moses; they doubted God. Even though they loved their freedom, they longed for the familiarity of Egypt more than the uncertainty of the days ahead.

And because of their response, the journey that could have taken weeks became a wandering that lasted 40 long, difficult years. They, not the devil, aborted God's plan. Therefore, they walked in circles for 40 years. They retraced the same steps year after year.

The same mountains.

The same valleys.
The same sand.
The same horizon.
We see this pattern everywhere today.

- The graduate who expected a dream job is still searching years later.
- The couple who thought they would have children quickly now wait and pray month after month.
- The leaders who expected doors to open find themselves in hidden seasons.
- The believer who expected breakthrough feels stuck in the process.

Time passes and nothing seems to change. You may have watched others advance while you are still behind. The wilderness often feels like delay. But heaven calls it preparation.

Forty years in the wilderness was never God's best for the Israelites. It was never His original intention for them to get derailed and blow up the original plan. God was going to use the 12 to 13 weeks of travel time to correctly reveal to them His matchless power, perfect love, zealous oversight, His nature, goodness, and strength. In this process, God had hoped through numerous revelations He would actually prepare them mentally, emotionally, and spiritually how to live continuously in His favor and how to conquer the enemies they would face.

For example, for the Israelites to thrive, God graciously revealed to them His standard of expected conduct. He summoned Moses to the top of the mountain and gave the people the Ten Commandments. The words on those tablets were not suggestions but actual mandates. They dealt with man's relationship with man and man's relationship with God. God clearly revealed that if the people fully adhered to the Ten Commandments, their obedience would grant them His ongoing protection, promotion, and prosperity.

God wanted to prepare them for the next season of their life. What exactly was that next? They would be given the Promised

Land that flowed with milk and honey; however, they would have to drive out its current inhabitants.

Again, the wilderness was not the destination; it was to be a tool God used to prepare them for the new land. And because of misunderstanding the ways and purpose of God, God would not let them advance and possess their new land.

WHAT GOD DOES IN THE WILDERNESS

God does some of His deepest work in the wilderness. It is a place of isolation and preparation.

The following is what I have discovered why God takes us into the wilderness:

- He teaches dependence.
- He reveals Himself in new ways.
- He builds endurance.
- He develops trust.
- He removes the residue of Egypt from the heart.

Let me add: It is critical that we know God has not changed. There are times and seasons God will intentionally dry up the water hole and place us in the wilderness. And, He does this not for punishment, but refinement. It is a training ground for those He loves. God does not waste wilderness seasons. Not one day. Not one step. Not one tear. It is a divine moment, orchestrated by heaven, so we can get a revelation and understanding of who God is and what He can do.

It is in these moments, if we look closely enough and listen carefully, God will reveal Himself to us in new ways. The wilderness is designed for our specific assignment. It is a place of preparation.

Embrace the season. The wilderness is not where your story ends. It is where your strength begins.

16

THE CRAB AND THE EAGLE

Growth often feels like progress. Movement. Momentum. Measurable improvement. We love seasons when prayers are answered quickly, doors open easily, and strength seems to increase by the day. In this time we feel loved, validated, and accepted.

But sometimes growth looks like loss. It looks like slowing down, being hidden, or even abandonment. It can feel like doors closing, routines changing, or familiar strengths fading. In those moments, it is easy to assume something has gone wrong. We wonder if we missed God, failed Him, or lost ground.

Yet some of the most important growth in our lives happens in seasons that do not look like progress at all. They feel quieter, slower, and more uncomfortable.

You are left to wonder, *What is going on?*

Have you been in this place before? I certainly have, more times than I can count.

These seasons are often misunderstood and misdiagnosed as failure, distance from God, or spiritual decline. In reality, they may be something very different from what our emotions are telling us. They may be a season of molting.

What Is Molting? Molting is the periodic shedding of an outer layer, for example, feathers, skin, hair, or an exoskeleton so that new growth can emerge. It is a normal part of life for birds, reptiles, insects, and crustaceans. Without this process, their development and growth stop. Many creatures molt. But two in particular teach us powerful lessons about spiritual transformation: the crab and the eagle.

THE CRAB: GROWTH REQUIRES BREAKING

Crabs and lobsters live inside hard shells that protect them from predators. These shells serve them well, at least for a season. But the shell that once protected them eventually becomes the very thing that limits them.

Crabs can only grow by molting. Their rigid exoskeleton must split open so a larger shell can form.

Dr. Stephen Sulkin, marine biologist, Western Washington University, explains it plainly: "Crabs grow only by molting. Without shedding the old shell, the animal cannot increase in size or repair accumulated damage."[27]

Growth requires breaking.

During molting, the crab becomes extremely vulnerable. It hides beneath rocks or buries itself in the ocean floor to escape the seeing eyes of its predators. In addition, during this phase, the crab is unable to defend itself; it simply waits for the new shell to harden. Marine ecologist Dr. Carl Wilson calls molting, "The most vulnerable and energetically expensive phase of a crab's life cycle."[28] Think about that. This phase of molting requires great energy and is costly. At no point in a crab's life is it more vulnerable to predators than at this phase. Life literally hangs in the balance.

Science concludes: without molting, the crab cannot grow. Without shedding, damage cannot be repaired. Without surrender, progress stops.

What once protected the crab eventually restricts it.

THE EAGLE: RENEWAL REQUIRES RELEASE

The eagle, one of Scripture's most repeated symbols of strength, is one of creation's greatest teachers when it comes to understanding the value of seasons and transitions.

Over time, an eagle's feathers become worn, heavy, and damaged. With a wingspan of up to 8 feet, dirt and oil accumulate, and flight becomes harder. The eagle has difficulty soaring to extreme heights; its speed decreases, and its overall efficiency declines.

Without renewal, the king of the skies would eventually be grounded. Is it still an eagle? Absolutely. However, the eagle's majesty is diminished. So once each year, the eagle goes through an arduous process called molting. It sheds old feathers so stronger ones can grow.

Ornithologist Dr. Jerome Jackson explains: "Eagles molt gradually over several years. It is a strategic process of renewal that prepares the bird for longevity and sustained flight."[29] Did you catch that? "It is a strategic process." The suffering and inconvenience, the disfiguring, and the isolation prepare the bird for durability and presence. Molting is a gift to the eagle, even though the eagle may resent it.

During this time, the eagle can still fly, but not as well as before. Its strength is limited, and its endurance is drastically reduced. In addition, its activity slows down, and the bird has to be calculated in its movements.

The eagle instinctively knows what we often resist—without releasing what is worn and weathered, it cannot rise into what is next.

By all standards, molting is slow. Hidden. Quiet. Painful.

The eagle embraces the moments ahead and faithfully perches and waits while unseen renewal takes place. This process does not take a few days; it can last months. During this span of time, the bird is more vulnerable to disease, stress, and even predators.

During this season the eagle looks and feels weaker. Its body seems to be deformed and diseased. However, looks do not tell the whole story. What is going on internally will eventually affect the exterior. While it looks tattered and defeated, it is actually being renewed. What appears to be decline is preparation. And with every passing day its body is being renovated. Eventually, it will emerge much stronger and more capable than before.

SPIRITUAL MOLTING—WHEN STRENGTH FEELS WEAK

Spiritually, molting seasons feel confusing. Your life seems to become tangled, emotions run high, and your areas of comfort are disrupted, if not altogether removed. You feel uncovered and vulnerable. You still love God. You still believe. You continue to read the Word, but things feel different. Something seems to be off. Even with the most seasoned, doubt can creep in. In addition, prayer feels ineffective. His voice quiets. You feel as if you are in a chamber of darkness. Any spiritual momentum seems to come to a crawl.

It feels like loss, but it is actually renovation. God is not removing His presence. He is enlarging your capacity.

Molting requires patience.

If a crab leaves shelter too early, it is certain death. If an eagle resists the process, it becomes weaker and never fully recovers from it. The physical development of both the crab and eagle is directly tied to this hidden season. Our temptation is to resist the process or to rush through it or, worse yet, quit.

Whatever you do, *do not panic!* This will soon pass. It will not last forever. Surrender your will to God and submit to the process. In the end, you will be glad you did.

17

IT IS NOT A VIDEO GAME

We live in a world obsessed with levels. Everything around us is built on progression, promotion, and advancement. Take the airline industry. The more you fly, the higher your status becomes. For example, the airline I use, Delta Airlines, has Silver, Gold, Platinum, and Diamond levels. With each new level comes new benefits, priority boarding, better seats, lounge access, upgrades, and special treatment. Why? Because loyalty and consistency earn you privileges, the more you fly, the higher your status and perks.

Hotels work the same way. Stay enough nights, and suddenly you move from "basic member" to "elite guest." The same room becomes a different experience. You may get free upgrades, early check-in, and even late checkouts without penalty. And in some cases you may even get a designated parking place.

Even credit cards have tiers. Spend more and you earn more points. Coffee shops even have levels—buy enough lattes and eventually the barista hands you one for free.

Most people strive to get to the next level. They want the next.

The global video game industry now generates more than $184 billion annually, and more than three billion people worldwide regularly play video games.[30] In the United States alone, two-thirds of adults play, and the average gamer is in their 30s.[31] This is no longer a niche hobby for teenagers; it is a cultural framework. And the average gamer spends from seven to ten hours every week playing.[32]

Furthermore, many teenagers spend two to three hours every day in virtual worlds built around one central idea—get to the next level. Their aim is to:

- Level up
- Unlock achievements
- Advance their character
- Gain new abilities
- Beat the next boss

Game designers understand this principle better than most. They intentionally build reward systems that keep players chasing progress.[33] The entire experience is engineered around advancement, visibility, recognition, and achievement.

You start at level one with basic tools, limited access, and simple assignments. But every task you complete, every villain defeated, every mission accomplished earns status and experience points. Slowly, the process bar fills, and suddenly, you *level up.*

Along the way you receive badges. Achievements. Trophies. Rankings. And you skyrocket up the leaderboard. Our brains are wired to love progress. We love visible movement. We love measurable advancement. We love knowing we are getting somewhere. It gives us a sense of accomplishment. Progress, especially in a video game, can become addictive.

The next few paragraphs and chapters challenge the way we think about spiritual growth. Many believers unknowingly approach their walk with God like a game, measuring progress by visibility, achievement, and recognition. Constantly striving to go higher.

WE HAVE TO CHANGE OUR MINDSET

This "level up" mindset has woven its way inside the Church. Which explains why we hear this phrase so often: "I'm going to the next level." Or, "New level, new devils."

I understand what people mean when they say it. Their hearts are usually sincere. But our walk with God is not a video game. Spiritual growth is not about unlocking spiritual achievements. It is not about earning upgrades. It is not about advancing to the next stage of visibility. It is about transformation. Expansion. Enlargement. Maturity. Trustworthiness.

KINGDOM MATH IS DIFFERENT

The language inside the church beltway often sounds like this:

- Addition
- Multiplication
- Increase
- Higher levels

These words are not wrong, but they are often misunderstood and could lead people into constant frustration and despair. This mindset says, "I could be more effective if I were more visible." Or, "I need more followers." And, "I need to get my name out so people will recognize my anointing." Too many of us have adopted the mindset of "I need to increase."

The kingdom of God runs on an entirely different math system. Kingdom math is not addition by promotion. It is increase by surrender. It is not climbing up. It is laying down. This is why John the Baptist gave us the clearest equation in Scripture: *"He must increase, but I must decrease"* (John 3:30 NKJV).

There it is. Clear as mountain river water. Decrease. Getting smaller. Going lower. Humility.

Spiritual effectiveness does not grow because we scratch and claw our way upward. It grows because we allow God to remove more of what stands in His way.

This is not about going up.

This is about giving up.

FORMATION, NOT ELEVATION

Scripture tells us we are being transformed *"from glory to glory"* (2 Corinthians 3:18 NKJV). Notice the language: transformation, not promotion. God is not trying to upgrade your platform, nor is He working to increase your number of followers. He is trying to conform your character.

And our pursuit must be the same—to be more like Him.

Again, this is not a new level. It is addition by subtraction. It is increase by removal.

What God is after is not elevation—it is formation.

And formation takes time.

It takes process.

It takes surrender.

It takes seasons.

And unlike a video game—there is no cheat code to spiritual maturity.

I believe 2 Corinthians 3:18, along with many others, teaches the value of a transformational process designed to make us like Jesus. Without the ongoing, conforming work of the Holy Spirit, we eventually become stuck. Our walk with God can drift into routine, stagnation, and ineffectiveness. But when we allow the process of spiritual metamorphosis to unfold, it reshapes not only what we do, but who we are.

SIGNS YOU MAY BE TREATING YOUR WALK WITH GOD LIKE A VIDEO GAME

- You are not impacted by the simplicity of the Word of God but seek out new emotional experiences.
- You want to have new encounters in God without maturing in your faith.
- You desire more of God, but are unwilling to give Him more.

- You compare your journey to others' journeys and seek to have what they have without going through what they went through to receive it.
- You long for impact and influence but ignore the call for purity.

I have cautioned you before, but I must do it again: this process of becoming more like Jesus is not quick, and it is rarely easy. At times it is difficult. At times it is painful. At times it feels slow and invisible. Yet in the end, it is always worth it.

Spiritual growth is not an upgrade; it is a renovation. We are encouraged to go from glory to glory, strength to strength, and faith to faith. This is not the next level; it is maturity.

One of God's goals is your spiritual expansion, an enlargement of your inner life so you can stand under, and operate under, a greater weight of glory without collapsing beneath it. Glory is not light; it is heavy. Again, 2 Corinthians 3:18 implies we go from the current weight of God's presence to a greater weight of God's presence. The amount of glory we can carry is up to us. God delights in giving you as much of His weight as your flesh can carry.

God is preparing you for something big, real big. Bigger than what you have imagined. However, one thing is necessary, He needs your footing to go deeper. Every engineer knows that enlargement without a proper foundation and solid footings inevitably leads to collapse. God digs deep before He builds high.

The good news: The process of God, when allowed to fulfill its purpose, enables us to enlarge our territory safely. As the base widens, territory expands. As the foundation deepens, authority increases. Our goal is not to reach the next level; our goal is to be prepared for all He has for us to do.

The kingdom of God is not a game; there are no shortcuts, and there are no cheat codes. There are no instant upgrades. The contrary is true; it often takes focused effort, discipline, and at times pain in order to mature. In a video game, you chase levels. You seek to conquer and advance. In the kingdom, you embrace surrender. In a video game, progress is instant and visible. In the kingdom, progress is slow and often hidden.

In a video game, the goal is to win. In the kingdom, the goal is to become like Jesus. And that transformation is worth every season, every surrender, and every step of the process.

18

THE DEVIL SAT CLOSE BY

A 2016 study by the Barna Group found that only 35 percent of Americans believe that satan is a real being, while the majority view him as either symbolic or are unsure.[34]

However, we know he is a real and viable entity.

The devil watches. He is an opportunistic foe with a remarkable skill for deception. He is a keen observer as he studies patterns and learns the rhythms of our movements. He knows our tendencies as he keeps a watchful eye on our reactions, responses, and interactions. In fact, I would even say satan is highly skilled at recognizing every weakness I have, we have.

Satan has been examining human tendencies since the beginning of time. Picture the moment in the Garden of Eden. Adam and Eve move freely through a perfect world. No pain. No fear. No shame. Only peace, beauty, and communion with God. Yet somewhere nearby, satan quietly watches. God had given only one clear instruction to the new couple—do not eat from that one tree.

Scripture does not suggest Eve sprinted toward the tree in rebellion. More likely, the moment unfolded slowly. Their curiosity grew, and interest in the forbidden tree lingered. The longer they stayed, the more the boundary blurred. As each of us knows, temptation is subtle, deceiving, and it usually begins with proximity.

Eve contemplated her moves, her options. She may have struggled greatly, and perhaps her spirit inside of her said, "Walk away. Don't do this." In addition, in her mind she kept hearing the voice of God saying, "Do not go near, do not touch!"

Satan did not drag Eve to the tree, nor did he force the fruit into her hand. He kept a keen eye on her every move. He simply waited for an opening, and when she moved close enough, he stepped into the conversation.

It was a conversation that was never meant to take place. However, it did, and satan had a few short minutes to present his case. He was compelling as he entered into a philosophical discussion that appealed to Eve's feelings, appetite, passions, and pursuits. He questioned God's true intentions for her life. He laid down what seemed to be an irresistible offer—and she took it.

It is worth repeating that satan waited patiently for a small opening, which is all he needed. He did not strike her with overwhelming demonic power, place her under a spell, or release a legion of demons upon her. He simply suggested how life would be better if she would indulge herself and look out for her own best interests.

Old Testament scholar Dennis F. Kinlaw described the strategy of the enemy with piercing clarity: "Satan disguises submission to himself under the ruse of personal autonomy. He never asks us to become his servants. Never once did the serpent say to Eve, 'I want to be your master.' The shift in commitment is never from Christ to evil; it is always from Christ to self. And instead of his will, self-interest now rules, and what I want reigns. And that is the essence of sin."[35]

I do not believe Eve sinned because she hated God; no, she sinned because she relaxed her watchfulness. Furthermore, I do not think she woke up that morning wanting to sabotage the beautiful work of God nor condemn all mankind to hardship, suffering, and eventually to hell. It was not on her radar at all. Not to oversimplify the matter, but she let her guard down and the enemy pounced on the opportunity. The rest is history.

Derek Prince, international Bible teacher, wrote: "Satan can do nothing unless we give him the ground. But once ground is given, he will exploit it to the full."[36] Prince's wording, "ground is given," is his theological way of describing legal access. Satan has limitations and cannot force entry, but he is relentless in waiting for an invitation. He seeks out an open door. And when the invitation is given, even slightly, he moves quickly and decisively. And the devastation and defeat that follows is brutal.

And if we are honest, Eve's story is a lot like our story. Most believers do not wake up in the morning intending to bring destruction into their lives or the lives of those they love. They have no intention of giving in to sin, mismanaging God's grace, power, or His will for their lives.

But again, satan is observant; he watches our movements over time. He notices when prayer becomes rushed and, even worse, a taxing burden, inconvenient. He sees when worship becomes more of a duty rather than a delight. He watches as we move into service as an obligation rather than a kingdom opportunity to help others.

As a good hunting dog has a keen sense of smell and can detect its game, satan can tell when our resolve is less than strong and when weariness begins to settle into the bones. He listens for tone shifts, when gratitude gives way to grumbling, when humility turns into entitlement, when joy quietly leaks out, and offense slips in unnoticed.

Scripture calls him *"a roaring lion, seeking whom he may devour."* The language is interesting in this verse. It does not say whom he *must* devour, but whom he *may* devour. That means opportunity matters. Timing matters. Condition matters. A lion does not attack the strongest animal in the herd. He waits. He circles. He studies the limp in the walk. He looks for vulnerabilities. Practically, satan observes the missed services, he notices priorities have shifted, he sees the isolation from the herd. He calmly waits until the conditions are right. Every move he takes is calculated.

The devil rarely attacks too early. There is one fruit of the Spirit he has mastered: patience. He will wait years and decades if that is what it takes to apprehend you. He waits until you are tired enough to compromise, hurt enough to rationalize, and alone enough to be vulnerable. He moves in decisively, not loudly, but with great precision. His goal is isolation, which leads to defeat.

This is why responding correctly to each season cannot be undervalued. Understanding the season matters so deeply. I have witnessed with my own eyes that many believers fall not because they do not love Jesus or lack anointing, but because they misread the stage they were in. They thought their weariness was harmless, their small offense was insignificant, and their break from ministry and service was a necessary sabbatical.

But the spiritual life moves in seasons and cycles. There are seasons for pressing forward, seasons for resting, seasons for pruning, and seasons for rebuilding. Wisdom is not only knowing what God is doing, but recognizing when He is doing it. When we misinterpret a pruning season as rejection, or a refining season as failure, we often respond in ways that create distance instead of growth.

And guess what?

The enemy sees our misevaluations and thrives when we misunderstand our season. He whispers that nothing is happening, that God has withdrawn, that stepping back will not matter. Don't believe him!

Every season carries an invitation. Some seasons call us to press in, others call us to guard what God has already done. Discernment is the difference between drifting and advancing. When we learn to recognize the season, we respond correctly, and when we respond correctly, we continue moving forward in God's cycle of growth.

19

INCREASE YOUR USABILITY

I say this carefully and not with a spirit of judgment, but with deep concern: many believers live their entire lives without ever becoming fully usable in the hands of God. That truth is uncomfortable, but ignoring it would be far more dangerous. Perhaps the greatest tragedy in the Christian life is not failure, but unused potential.

I truly believe most believers genuinely desire to be used by God. The desire is real. The hunger is sincere. The willingness is there. But desire alone is not the same as readiness. Think about someone who has always dreamed of becoming a doctor. Their heart may be set on helping people. They may feel compassion for the sick. They may even feel called to the medical field. But no hospital would ever hand them a scalpel and say, "Start performing surgery."

Desire is great and it needs to be celebrated. It is a good starting point. However, before someone can be trusted with patients, the person must go through years of training, testing, refining, and supervised practice. Their desire is not questioned, but their preparation is required. The issue is not whether they *want* to help people. The issue is whether they are *ready* to help people.

The same is true spiritually. The desire to be used by God is commendable. Yet desire must be matched with preparation. There are conditions, character requirements, and refining processes that must take place before we can steward what God wants to entrust to us and meet the needs of the people He wants to reach.

God is not looking for perfect people, but He is looking for prepared people. And sanctification is the loving process through which He prepares us.

Second Timothy 2:20-21 (NKJV) says:

> *But in a great house there are not only vessels of gold and silver, but also of wood and clay, some for honor and some for dishonor. Therefore if anyone cleanses himself from the latter, he will be a vessel for honor, sanctified and useful for the Master, prepared for every good work.*

THE INVITATION

The beauty of this truth is both sobering and hopeful: we have a part to play in the process. We actually get a say in the degree to which God uses us in His kingdom.

Paul told young Timothy that in a great house there are vessels of *gold and silver,* but also vessels of *wood and clay.* Some are used for special purposes, others for common use.

Then comes the invitation: "If anyone cleanses himself, he will be a vessel for honor, sanctified and useful for the Master, prepared for every good work." Notice the language carefully. The passage does not say God is unwilling to use people.

On the contrary, it reveals that God desires to use people in His kingdom, but not at the same level. Greater responsibility is given to those who are willing to be cleansed. In other words, the material and assignment of the vessel is not permanent; it is *formed through sanctification.*

WOOD OR GOLD?

We choose whether we remain wood and clay, or become gold and silver. Without question, most believers long to be used by God, and they can be. Even the wood and clay in the Master's house have a purpose. However, the gold and silver vessels are allowed to go places that wood and clay are not allowed to go. They carry greater responsibility and are used in entirely different environments.

This truth is both humbling and empowering. It is humbling because it removes our excuses. It is empowering because it gives us hope. Our usefulness is not determined by talent, personality, platform, or opportunity. It is determined by our willingness to cooperate with the cleansing work of God.

Paul makes the progression unmistakably clear:

Cleanse → Sanctified → Useful → Prepared.

God does not skip steps.

We often want usefulness first. God insists on cleansing. We want high-impact ministries, but God requires sanctification. We want kingdom effectiveness on public display. God invites you to meet with Him in private so He can work on the secrets of the heart.

Let us not forget that gold and silver are refined in fire. They are heated, purified, and hammered into form before they are placed into service.

The promise is breathtaking: *"If anyone cleanses himself...he will be a vessel for honor."* The door is open to anyone. Not the most gifted. Not the most educated. Not the most connected. Anyone.

The determining factor is not someone's ability, but their submission to the process of sanctification. And this is the great revelation of sanctification: God is not trying to disqualify us. He is preparing us for His use.

The question is no longer, "Does God want to use me?" The real question becomes, "How much preparation am I willing to embrace so that He can?"

THE FIRE OF PREPARATION

Hebrews 12:27 (NIV) reminds us that God allows shaking *"so that what cannot be shaken may remain."* This is the uncomfortable truth about sanctification: it is not fun, nor is it easy. Things we justified begin to surface. Hidden debris is exposed. At times this process is painful. At times it is deeply humbling. At times it can even feel embarrassing. But Scripture refuses to let us misunderstand the purpose.

Malachi paints the picture with startling clarity: "*...For He will be like a refiner's fire or a launderer's soap. He will sit as a refiner and purifier of silver; he will purify the Levites and refine them like gold and silver...*" (Malachi 3:2-3 NIV).

Notice the posture of God in this passage; He sits as a refiner. He is not in a hurry. He is attentive. He is intentional. He is committed to the process, and nothing escapes His eye as He watches every flicker of the flame. Recently, I was at a silversmith's shop. He was making a knife from scratch. I watched him carefully take a piece of metal and place it in the fire. After a few moments with thongs he would remove the metal from the fire and begin to hit it with a hammer on an anvil. After a few seconds of pounding the metal, He would place it back in the fire. He did this repeatedly until it was formed into the shape of knife and then sharpened and ready to use. Two things were constant—fire and pressure.

Here is what I know: Refining is hot. Refining is slow. Refining is intentional.

As A.W. Tozer, well-known Christian pastor and author, wisely observed, "God cannot fill what He cannot cleanse."

When we allow the Holy Spirit to expose and remove the hidden debris in our lives, we are positioning ourselves for greater usefulness. We become vessels capable of carrying a greater weight of glory.

Hebrews 12:1 (NKJV) describes this refining process: "*...let us lay aside every weight, and the sin which so easily ensnares us, and let us run with endurance the race that is set before us.*"

The refining fire removes unnecessary weight. This can be difficult for our flesh, but it is absolutely necessary to eliminate whatever hinders our walk, growth, and maturity. Scripture calls us to "*lay aside every weight and the sin which so easily ensnares us*" (Hebrews 12:1 NKJV). Notice the distinction: all sin is weight, but not all weight is sin.

Some things are not evil; they are simply heavy. And anything heavy will slow a runner.

- Indifference is a weight.
- Distractions are a weight.

- Unresolved offense is a weight.
- Bitterness is a weight.
- Unforgiveness is a weight.
- Pride is a weight.
- Fear of man is a weight.
- Busyness without purpose is a weight.
- Comfort is a weight.
- Familiarity with God's presence is a weight.
- Compromise is a weight.
- Spiritual laziness is a weight.
- Endless entertainment is a weight.
- Constant noise is a weight.
- Divided affections are a weight.

And sometimes even good things—relationships, opportunities, responsibilities, and ambitions—can become weights when they occupy a place God never intended them to hold.

Some believers are not bound by chains; they are slowed by baggage. The refining process targets anything that keeps us from running freely. God instructs us to remove whatever slows or restricts movement, clouds vision, or drains spiritual strength. He is not trying to make life smaller, He is trying to make us lighter. Lighter is much better.

What feels like loss is often God removing resistance. What feels like subtraction is actually preparation. The refining fire is determined to remove anything and everything that slows us down so we can run the race set before us with endurance and freedom.

It is the prayer of the psalmist becoming reality: *"Search me, O God, and know my heart: try me, and know my thoughts: And see if there be any wicked way in me, and lead me in the way everlasting"* (Psalm 139:23-24 KJV).

When a church embraces this prayer, when believers invite this searching, when the Spirit is welcomed to reveal what lies beneath the surface, something extraordinary happens—the vessel becomes usable to the Master.

Again, the process can be painful; therefore, we must remember that sanctification is not punishment. It is preparation. God is not reducing you; He is refining you. He is not setting you aside; He is setting you apart. He is not limiting your future, He is enlarging your capacity.

The very process that feels like loss is actually increasing your usability. And one day you will look back and realize that the season that exposed you was the season that prepared you.

20

BATTLE TESTED, BATTLE READY

The Purple Heart is the oldest military decoration still awarded to soldiers by the president of the United States. Its origins trace back to George Washington's Badge of Military Merit, a symbol of courage and sacrifice in service to one's country.

The Purple Heart is not given for good intentions or strong training. It is awarded to those who have paid a price. Among the qualifications are:

- Wounded in combat
- Killed in action
- Taken prisoner by enemy forces

It is a medal marked by sacrifice.

I carry a deep sense of honor when I think about my grandfather, a World War II veteran who received the Purple Heart. He was wounded while advancing under enemy fire—an act of courage he never spoke about. He carried his memories quietly, but I will always honor his sacrifice.

Over the years, I have spoken with many men and women who have been to war. Their stories differ, but one truth remains constant: they are never the same afterward. The sights, the sounds, the smells remain etched into memory.

War leaves a permanent mark.

Yet there is something remarkable about a tested soldier. They think differently. They live differently. They see danger sooner. They value life more deeply. Something inside them has been forged by experience.

Training can teach discipline and skill, but battle teaches realities that training alone never can. Drill instructors work hard to simulate combat conditions, but simulation is never the same as live fire. When combat becomes real, a soldier learns in real time, and from that moment forward, fights with a deeper level of understanding.

Soldiers who have endured live gunfire, exhaustion, fear, and confusion and refused to retreat emerge with hardened instincts and situational awareness. What once startled them no longer does. They have been remade by the fight.

War exposes both strengths and weaknesses. Battle-tested soldiers quickly learn where they are vulnerable and learn to guard those areas carefully. Experience trains judgment. Through victories and losses, they learn when to advance, when to hold, and when to wait.

Seasoned soldiers not only know how to follow orders, but they also understand why obedience matters. They know that missions succeed or fail based on coordinated obedience. When a soldier ignores orders, the consequences extend far beyond that one individual; in all honesty, it could be catastrophic. In addition, unit cohesion breaks down.

Each soldier's position is connected to another's safety. When one person fails, others must compensate. Flanks become exposed. Positions weaken. Trust erodes. No one in the group knows who has their back. Once cohesion fractures, the entire unit becomes vulnerable. More casualties are likely the result.

Veterans understand something civilians often overlook: when one soldier stops fighting, the entire mission is endangered.

In warfare, success often depends on timing and synchronized movement. One delay can collapse the objective. One failure can multiply casualties.

One person's retreat can affect the entire war.

THE WAR OF SANCTIFICATION

The Sanctification Phase is a war. It is a war against our flesh. A war against pride. A war against hidden compromise. A war against shallow faith. A war against divided loyalty.

In this war, at times there is profound confusion, exhaustion, and even degrees of fear. During the Stimulation Phase of revival, believers often rely on ideals and hopeful declarations:

"I'll trust God."

"I'll stand firm."

"I won't quit!"

"Nothing can stop me."

But in the Sanctification Phase, those declarations are tested, and our slogans meet reality. Our faith is truly measured, and our endurance gets challenged. In reality, this season locates you. You no longer imagine how you would respond; you discover how you actually respond when the bullets begin to fly.

Sanctification reveals what stimulation concealed.

Believers who endure sanctification come out changed; they walk differently. They are wiser and speak more carefully. They judge others less harshly, and they walk with a greater degree of humility. They possess a deeper gratitude for the sweet things of God. They understand weakness and vulnerabilities. They depend on God more completely.

This newness positions us to experience more of God's glory. We come forth broken but not destroyed; refined, but not ruined. Therefore, now we are able to carry more of the weight of God. Our eyes are keener, our spirits more aware. Our hearts are softened, and our love for others has multiplied.

The improvements the Lord makes in our hearts during the arduous Sanctification Phase prepare us for the next thing God wants to do in us personally, our future assignments. Our willingness to keep advancing through the process has now made room for more—more responsibility, more power, more influence, more authority. It increases our capacity to host the Lord well alongside our fellow soldiers.

STEADYING THE NEW SOLDIERS

When new soldiers first encounter the battlefield, they are often overwhelmed by the noise, confusion, the screams, death, the smells, and the overall violence of war. Veteran soldiers understand this.

They know what fear feels like. They remember their first battle. And because of that experience, they help steady the inexperienced. They offer comforting words such as:

"I've been there."

"This hurts, but it won't destroy you."

"Stay steady."

"You're not alone."

"Don't panic."

"Don't quit now."

"Victory comes after this."

The same is true in revival.

Believers who have endured sanctification become stabilizers for others entering the same season. They know the signs and recognize the pressure this season brings. They understand the confusion. They become voices of calm in seasons of shaking.

WARRIORS ARE MADE

Warriors are not born, they are made. Anybody can put on a uniform and pretend to be a soldier, talk like a soldier, and even carry a weapon like a soldier. But true soldiers are fighters. And the Sanctification Phase takes us from raw new recruits into effective kingdom warriors. God never wastes a battle or a season. Everything has a purpose.

Every believer who endures the Sanctification Phase receives something far greater than a medal.

They receive a layer of necessary experience. They mature. And though there is no ribbon to pin on their chest, heaven recognizes them as soldiers who are more usable and dependable.

PART FOUR

THE SHOCK AND AWE PHASE

21

YOU GRADUATED!

God does not pass you to the next phase without you passing certain tests, overcoming trials, performing tasks, and conquering temptations. In the sanctification process ,you will undergo trials, tests, and be confronted with tasks. In this phase, the tests you undergo prove to you and God what you know. The trials you face will reveal what you can endure, and the tasks reveal what you can do. All of this helps prepare you for the next season.

Coming out of the Sanctification Phase is not an emotional rebound but a capacity increase in your heart and soul. You emerge wiser, more broken, tender, and more sensitive to the promptings of the Holy Spirit.

Graduation time. Now you are ready for the next thing God wants to do in you, around you, and through you. Graduating out of the prior phase qualifies you to carry more weight of His glory. In addition, it allows you to become more useful to God. Yes, that is correct. *"In a great house…if anyone cleanses himself…he will be a vessel for honor…useful to the Master…"* (2 Timothy 2:20-21 NKJV).

Something fundamental shifts inside the heart. Before sanctification, many believers quietly ask, "How close can I get to sin and still maintain my relationship with Jesus?"

After sanctification, the question changes, "How close can I get to Him?"

The Shock and Awe Phase is a beautiful season. You are able to see and feel again. In this phase, you get to witness heaven touch the earth in unusual power demonstrations. The difference is weight. The difference is depth. The difference is understanding.

For example, the power that rested around the people in phase one now begins to work through them. Their vision is clearer, their discernment is sharper, and the giftings in their life become more expressive and easier to activate. Authority in the Spirit becomes more evident as God has prepared His children for the deeper work.

Not only does the frequency of miracles increase, but people witness miracles that were not seen in the prior days. The "wonders" of the Lord increase in quantity and quality.

THE RETURN OF THE PRESENCE

One of the most satisfying aspects of this phase is the renewed appreciation for the presence of God. Why? You see again. You feel again. But now you cherish it differently because you thought you lost it.

Those who have passed through sanctification understand the value of nearness. The presence of God is no longer assumed; it is treasured. Like a husband who almost lost his marriage or a patient who nearly lost his life, they value what others take for granted.

POWER AFTER PURIFICATION

The Shock and Awe Phase stands upon the foundation of the first two phases—stimulation and sanctification. Many people embrace the Stimulation Phase, however, few endure the season of sanctification. Therefore, only a remnant enters the Shock and Awe Phase.

The Sanctification Phase often lasts weeks or months and feels like a wilderness. Many grow discouraged and return to familiar patterns. Others assume something has gone wrong and abandon the process. But those who endure discover something extraordinary: God trusts purified vessels with greater power. He increases their influence and enlarges their usefulness.

It is as if heaven declares: "Now that you are prepared, I can entrust you with more."

Faith rises to a new level among those who graduate from the Sanctification Phase. Things that once seemed implausible suddenly become possible. Prayers that once felt inadequate and ineffective now seem to be heard. The power of God begins to expand in this phase, stretching the boundaries of what the people believed could happen.

It is worth noting that issues that would take months to manifest now manifest in only weeks; what normally would take weeks now happens in days. There is an unmistakable acceleration in the Spirit realm. Doors open faster. Answers come quicker. Direction becomes clear. God is not moving faster because He changed; He is moving faster because we are lighter and are now ready for our next assignment.

THE SHIFT IN PRAYER

Prayer meetings change in this phase. The people are battle-tested and now pray differently. They pray with focus and urgency. Things have shifted. There is a surge of boldness in the intercession; the timidity has melted away, and now declarations are made in great faith with full expectation that God will respond. Why? Because God has tried them, they came through the fire, and now they have a sense that heaven is leaning in and listening to the faintest request. They pray like Elijah on Mount Carmel. They pray like the early Church in Acts. They pray like Jacob, "I will not go until you bless me." They pray like people who have been through the fire and came out believing.

WHEN GLORY INTENSIFIES

In this phase, the weight of God's presence intensifies both personally and corporately. The worship services carry an even deeper presence. Our worship is more personal and engaging. Our ears listen more attentively when the Word of God is preached. Inside and outside the building, those who have passed through the Sanctification

Phase walk with a new authority as faith is strengthened. And once again, the people begin to sense they are standing inside a move of God rather than merely attending meetings.

SHOCK AND AWE

This phase deserves its name. Because when God begins to move through purified vessels, the effect is undeniable. Heaven invades, and miracles multiply.

Shock and awe is what happens when God entrusts prepared people with uncommon power. And those who endured the fire of sanctification suddenly realize:

- The fire was preparation.
- The wilderness was positioning.
- The silence was not abandonment,
- It was training for glory.

22

WHEN GLORY ARRIVES

As revival intensifies, it eventually leads to an encounter with the glory of God. At this point, something profound happens. Your awareness awakens. His holy light begins to penetrate every corner of your life. Nothing feels hidden. Every motive of your heart is revealed. Desires are uncovered. You begin to see yourself as you really are.

Hebrews 4:12 tells us the Word of God can divide soul and spirit, bone and marrow. Because the written Word can expose us this deeply, how much more does the unveiled glory of God lay bare everything within us that is unlike Him?

Throughout Scripture, encounters with God's glory always reveal the tension between His purity and the remnants of sin within us. When we embrace the purpose of God's glory, carnality becomes repulsive. Compromise becomes unbearable. Suddenly, you realize you are standing on holy ground. And like Moses, the only reasonable response is to remove your shoes, fall on your face, and draw as close to Him as you possibly can.

WHY PETER WANTED TO STAY

Knowing this helps us understand Peter's reaction on the Mount of Transfiguration. Overwhelmed by the nearness of heaven, Peter blurted out: *"Lord, it is good for us to be here; if You wish, let us make here three tabernacles: one for You, one for Moses, and one for Elijah"* (Matthew 17:4 NKJV).

Why did he suggest such a thing? At first glance, it certainly was a brassy request. I don't believe Peter was being disrespectful; however, he saw and felt something he had never encountered before. It was overwhelming to him, James, and John as they were experiencing unfiltered glory.

The moment was so sacred, so beautiful that he wanted to create a place to preserve the moment by building three tabernacles. He surmised that this encounter is too precious to experience just once. And if we are honest, we understand him completely. His heart was good, and I believe his intentions were pure; he did not want this moment to slip away.

This isn't the first time someone would linger to encounter the glory of God.

Moses would meet with God in what he called the "tent of meeting." It is recorded that while Moses was meeting with God, Joshua would linger just outside the entrance, unwilling to depart from that holy atmosphere, the glory that was present. Scripture tells us, *"So the Lord spoke to Moses face to face, as a man speaks to his friend. And he would return to the camp, but his servant Joshua the son of Nun, a young man, did not depart from the tabernacle"* (Exodus 33:11 NKJV).

Joshua positioned himself where the residue of glory remained. He refused to leave the atmosphere of God's presence. He lingered. And those who have tasted glory always do. It is a divine moment when heaven's reality presses on us, and no flesh can withstand it.

HEAVEN GUARDS WHAT IS SACRED

When someone truly experiences the glory, they step into a realm few humans have ever experienced. I remember a conversation I had with Pastor Phil Cameron shortly after the revival began at our church. He said, "Todd, it is a rare thing for the glory of God to touch the earth. It is not happening everywhere." Then he added,

"Because it is such a rare thing, when it does happen, God will send forth His angels to protect it!"

Why would angels be assigned to these moments? Because the glory of God is not ordinary.

It is holy, weighty, and transformative. It changes people, shifts atmospheres, and marks places. The Bible often tells how the glory even fills a room, like when the cloud filled the tabernacle, and the priests could not stand to minister (Exodus 40:34-35).

Charles Finney speaks about what happened when the glory of God fell during one of his meetings: "The very atmosphere seemed charged with the presence of God. I could hardly open my mouth in conversation before the Spirit fell upon those I spoke with, and they were immediately convicted and converted."[37]

The Bible repeatedly shows that angels are dispatched when God's glory touches the earth. Their assignment is not random. They guard sacred space.

For example, after humanity's fall, God stationed cherubim at the entrance of Eden to guard the way to the Tree of Life (Genesis 3:24). This was the first picture of heaven protecting holy ground. Eden was no longer ordinary territory; it had become a sacred space marked by divine visitation. As Old Testament scholar T. Desmond Alexander notes, "cherubim here function as 'custodians of sacred space,' marking the boundary between divine holiness and human brokenness."[38]

Later, when God instructed Moses to build the tabernacle, the mercy seat, the place where God's glory would rest, was overshadowed by cherubim (Exodus 25:18-22). Their wings stretched over the ark as a visual declaration that heaven guarded the place where God chose to dwell.

When Solomon built the temple, massive cherubim again filled the Holy of Holies (1 Kings 6:23-28). The message was unmistakable: wherever God's glory rests, heaven stands watch.

This pattern continues into the New Testament. At the empty tomb, angels were present where the glory of resurrection had just touched the earth (John 20:12). At the ascension, angels stood nearby as Jesus entered glory (Acts 1:10). Again and again, Scripture quietly shows angels stationed at moments when heaven and earth intersect.

Heaven does not treat God's manifest presence casually.

Neither should we.

23

THE MAN WHO REFUSED TO QUIT

In the 1968 Mexico City Olympics, the world witnessed one of the most unforgettable moments in Olympic history.

Surprisingly, it did not happen when Ethiopian runner Mama Wolfe crossed the finish line to win the gold medal. The moment that captured the heart of the world happened hours later, after the cameras were gone and the stadium had mostly emptied.

This is what happened. Seventy-five runners lined up for the marathon that day. Each athlete had trained for years to represent their family and their nation. Among them was a runner from Tanzania named John Stephen Akhwari.

When the starting gun sounded, the runners surged forward, setting into their rhythm. Then, without warning, disaster struck. As Akhwari fought for position, his legs tangled with another competitor, and he crashed violently to the ground. The fall was devastating. His shoulder was badly injured, and his knee was dislocated.

He was badly hurt. The medical personnel urged him to withdraw from the race. He refused. He dragged himself upright, even though he was limping, bandaged, and barely balanced; he continued the race. Every step was agony, but he kept running, driven by the defiant fire of a man who had already decided quitting was not an option.

Hours passed, and as the sun began to set over Mexico City, a whisper rippled through the remaining spectators in the Olympic stadium: "There's one more runner still out there." Many doubted the report, but it was true. The crowd had largely gone home; to them, the race was over. The gold medal was placed around the neck of Mamo Wolde of Ethiopia.

Long after the ceremony had ended and the television crews had packed up their equipment, one determined, wounded man was still hobbling, limping, dragging his swollen, injured leg mile after mile, attempting to make his way to the finish line.

Then he appeared.

As the day was surrendering to the night, Akhwari entered the stadium. There were no gold medals waiting. No cameras flashing. No roar of a packed crowd. Those still present stood to their feet in awe. The applause was thunderous. His stride was painfully broken, his face contorted with agony, his bandages soiled with dirt and blood. But every step was an undeniable declaration: "I refuse to surrender." Akhwari's entrance into that stadium was a moment in time that will never be forgotten. What they were witnessing was not athleticism or talent; it was determination in its most passionate form.

When reporters later asked him why he had not quit the race, John Stephen Akhwari offered one of the most iconic statements in Olympic history: "My country did not send me 5,000 miles to start the race; they sent me 5,000 miles to finish the race."[39]

STARTERS VERSUS FINISHERS

Anybody can start a race. Finishing is something entirely different. God does not celebrate starters; He crowns finishers. The apostle Paul understood this concept better than any other author of the Bible. Over and over, he observed the Christian life as a journey, a marathon, not a sprint. *"...let us run with patience the race that is set before us"* (Hebrews 12:1 KJV). The NKJV phrase used is *"run with endurance,"* which is the Greek word *hypomone*, meaning "steadfast perseverance under pressure—the ability to remain faithful when the weight of life presses hard against you.

Paul later wrote these words to his young son in the Lord, Timothy: *"I have fought the good fight, I have finished the race, I have kept the faith"* (2 Timothy 4:7 NKJV). Notice the order: I fought. I finished. I kept the faith.

This was not the language of someone who had lived an easy or comfortable life. The very opposite is true. Paul wrote these words after imprisonments, beatings, shipwrecks, snake bites, stonings, ejection, demonic attacks, and relentless opposition. Yet at the end of his journey, he did not celebrate comfort or success; he celebrated completion.

THE PRICE FOR LOOKING BACK

Human nature is to "pull back" when things become difficult. Jesus knew this and spoke into it. Jesus said, *"No one who puts a hand to the plow and looks back is fit for service in the kingdom of God"* (Luke 9:62 NIV).

To plow effectively, a farmer must look forward. Looking back creates crooked rows and an unpredictable harvest. This is unacceptable. The word translated *fit* can also mean useful. In other words—anyone who begins but constantly looks back cannot be fully effective in the kingdom. They are not trustworthy.

LISTEN WITH BOTH EARS

"Looking and pulling back" can no longer be an option for us. It cannot even enter our minds. Every time the enemy whispers to our ears for us to slow down, go back, and to rethink our commitment, we must respond with an overwhelming "NO! I WILL NOT LOOK BACK!" Jesus added in Revelation 2:10 (NKJV) that one of the potential crowns a believer receives in heaven is determined by finishing the entire race, *"Be faithful until death, and I will give you the crown of life."*

I need to remind you that there is a lot at stake. Paul urges us to *"Run in such a way that you may obtain it* [the prize]" (1 Corinthians 9:24 NKJV).

As in life, each race comes with obstacles, opposition, setbacks, unmet expectations, disappointments, difficulties, highs, and lows.

This is part of life and part of your walk with God. Our God didn't save you to simply take you to heaven, but to finish the race well. Our goal is to get to the place the apostle Paul came to, *"I have finished the race…."*

We all long to hear the words of Jesus on Judgment Day, *"Well done, good and faithful servant."* However, if we haven't been faithful, Jesus cannot and will not lie. Therefore, we must run the race, put our hand to the plow, and not look back.

HOW DO WE FINISH WELL?

All of us want to finish the Christian race well. None of us wants to quit; however, the enemy and life circumstances chip away at our faith, relationship with Christ, and our purpose.

Even though there are many things I could share here, I will reduce it to one thing: *endurance.*

Endurance is more than surviving hardship; it is the deep resolve to stay in love with God, aligned with Him when quitting would be easier. Endurance does not take on a passive posture; no, it is an active perseverance—it keeps moving, praying, serving, helping, loving, and attending. We all begin well with great intentions, but endurance keeps us in the fight even after being punched in the face.

We have learned via hard knocks that life is not always going to be easy, and we are going to face opposition. Our enemy is fierce and seeks to devour us. He does not fight by the rules. There will be opportunities to quit and walk away, to pull back. And the naturally seeing people would not blame you. However, Jesus expects more from us. He looks for wholehearted, undivided commitment. Remember, He said, *"No one who puts a hand to the plow and looks back is fit for service in the kingdom of God"* (Luke 9:62 NIV).

Many Bible translations, like the one in the NIV, use the word *fit* to describe one's position in the kingdom when they keep looking back or away from their role of plowing a field. As mentioned previously, God is not being cruel. He is revealing that if you plow a field and you get distracted and keep looking back, your rows will not be straight, you will be all over the place, and it will make it extremely difficult to gather in the harvest.

The Greek word for *fit* is *euthetos,* and according to Strong's Concordance, there are a few different words that could be used in this text other than *fit*. One of them is *useful*. I like this better, and I believe it is the more appropriate translation. In other words, their service will not be productive.

Take a look at these two versions of Luke 9:62—I think they get it right. The word *fit* that most translations use does not fully reveal what God is saying—I believe the best word is "useful."

> *Jesus answered, "Anyone who starts plowing and keeps looking back isn't worth a thing to God's kingdom!"* (Contemporary English Version)

> *Jesus said to him, "Anyone who starts to plow and then keeps looking back is of no use for the Kingdom of God"* (Good News Translation).

God expects us to push through the distractions, disappointments, offenses, excuses, and temptations in order to honor and represent Him correctly. The luxury to look back and to be in and out of service for the Lord is long gone. These are difficult days, and God is looking for faithful soldiers who will execute their roles with precision and endurance. Soldiers who have tenacity, grit, resilience, staying power. Is that you? Are you useful or do you keep looking back, easily offended, in and out, or up and down?

Remember Akhwari the marathon runner, "My country did not send me 5,000 miles to start the race…but to finish it."

PART FIVE
THE SERVICE PHASE

24

ARMY VERSUS AUDIENCE

We come now to the final cycle—Service.

Up to this point, God has been working deeply within us. He stirred our hearts in the Stimulation Phase. He has purified our lives in the Sanctification Phase. He has entrusted us with greater power and glory in the Shock and Awe Phase.

Revival is not solely about encounters; revival is also about deployment. God grows roots so He can extend His reach. His goal has never been the mere experience of revival; it has always been about greater fruitfulness.

True encounters with God serve a purpose greater than just the beautiful moment of personal transformation. Yes, the joy experienced and the internal healing that God poured out on you have a greater aim. Revival is a launching pad. The ultimate objective is missional release, both individually and corporately.

The touch of God that changed your life was never meant to stop with you. What God pours into you is designed to flow through you. This is the natural progression of revival—*from encounter to expression.*

Yet this is where many believers hesitate.

Why do so many people remain recipients but never become conduits? Why do some believers stay in the posture of "Fill me" but never move to "Send me"?

Part of the answer may be uncomfortable.

Many churches have unintentionally trained believers to see themselves as consumers rather than contributors, as attendees rather than participants, as audiences rather than soldiers. Instead of preparing believers for spiritual battle and kingdom expansion, we have sometimes taught them to evaluate church the same way they evaluate a product.

"How does this church meet my needs?"

"Do I like it here?"

"How does this church serve me?"

This consumer mindset is one of the greatest obstacles to sustained revival. A move of God cannot be sustained by spectators. Revival requires servants.

THE MANDATE THAT CHANGED EVERYTHING

In early 2013, I received a directive from the Lord that permanently altered my ministry. It came unexpectedly and with unmistakable clarity. The words echoed through my spirit with such force that I knew immediately something had shifted. God was realigning me with His heart.

Up to that point, I had been deeply invested in the church growth movement. I read everything I could find about increasing attendance. I searched for better methods, stronger systems, and more effective strategies to bring people into the building. I wanted people to hear the messages and experience what God was doing in our church.

My motives were not wrong. Many people were saved, and lives were changed. But looking back, I see that my focus had become too narrow.

Like many pastors, I concentrated heavily on attracting people and encouraging my congregation to invite others. But one of the hidden dangers of a consumer-driven model is that you can succeed in gathering crowds while failing to prepare disciples.

Not every church falls into this trap, but it is far more common than we would like to admit.

This emphasis produced a generation of churchgoers who learned to approach church the way they approach buying a car—evaluating features, preferences, and benefits.

"What does this church offer me?"

Then God spoke.

I was startled, but the moment was unmistakable. The words were clear and direct. Deep in my spirit I heard the Lord say, "Todd, do not build an audience. Build Me an army I can use."

Then again: "Don't build Me an audience—build Me an army."

Those words redefined everything. Let me be clear, He was not giving me a suggestion or saying, "Here is a good idea—take it or leave it." No, it was a command. His words on that day have reshaped my priorities, my leadership, and the direction of our entire church. That mandate has remained with me ever since, echoing in my heart like a constant call to plan for His children.

Revival is not about gathering an audience. Revival is about raising an army.

25

THE OVERFLOW OF REVIVAL

The Service Phase is marked by outward movement.

When revival reaches maturity, something begins to shift among the people. They no longer attend simply to receive. They come ready to give. Generosity increases. Sacrifice becomes normal, and opportunities to serve are no longer avoided—they are pursued and embraced with joy.

These manifestations are not forced programs or strategic initiatives. They are the natural result of transformed hearts. Broken people who have become benefactors of the grace and goodness of God cannot remain passive for long. Something inside them must move.

Those affected by revival begin to develop burdens for people they have never met and places they have never seen. Compassion surfaces for those who may have never heard the gospel, and they begin to feel the weight of eternity pressing upon their hearts. The awareness grows that souls hang in the balance and something must be done.

This is the missional overflow of revival. It just happens. It is not manufactured, and it is not a quick emotional response. It is deeper and more genuine.

One way to understand overflow is through the picture of pressure. When rain falls in the mountains, rivers begin to swell.

Eventually, the banks can no longer contain the rising water. The river spreads outward into surrounding fields and valleys. It does not ask permission. It does not wait for a committee meeting. It flows because pressure demands release.

Revival works the same way.

When God begins to pour out His Spirit, something builds inside His people. Love increases. Compassion deepens. Faith rises. Gratitude overflows. Eventually, the heart cannot contain what God has placed inside. It must flow outward. A revival that never overflows is not a healthy revival.

Life that does not reproduce eventually dies.

A SIGN THAT REVIVAL IS REAL

One of the clearest signs that revival is genuine is outward movement. Short-term mission involvement often doubles, sometimes even quadruples, during revival seasons. Evangelism becomes natural. Compassion ministries expand. Prayer for the lost intensifies. This is not theory, it is history.

The Welsh Revival of 1904 sent missionaries around the world within a few short years. The Moravian Revival in Herrnhut resulted in one of the greatest missionary movements in church history. The early Church in the book of Acts moved rapidly from Jerusalem into Judea, Samaria, and the ends of the earth. Real revival spreads. It always has and it always will.

IT HAPPENED TO US

I saw this happen in our own church.

Before revival, many believers struggled just to stay engaged. However, after revival began, they looked for opportunities to share the gospel. It was natural and did not have to be persuaded. They were compelled.

The North Georgia Revival developed a burden to spread what God is doing in the world. One of our outreaches was to the five Boroughs of New York City. We wanted to preach, worship, and baptize people in the darkest regions of New York City. It was the largest mission effort I have ever led. More than 300 people affiliated with our church and the North Georgia Revival descended upon the city.

This would never have been possible prior to revival. But when God touches a people deeply enough, staying comfortable becomes impossible. This outward movement, and others like it, is one of the clearest signs that revival is genuine. When revival is real, the love of God does not stagnate; it spreads.

REVIVAL WAS NEVER MEANT TO STAY IN ONE PLACE

Revival is never about benefiting a small group of people. God touches a congregation so that the congregation can touch the world. God does not want His move to be confined to the four walls of the church building. I am convinced revival is not complete until it moves beyond the walls of the church and into the streets, neighborhoods, and nations.

The book of Acts makes this unmistakably clear. The Spirit fell in Jerusalem, but the mission was always the world. Yes, Jerusalem was the birthplace, but the power and glory of Christ were never to be confined to one city, one people.

THE DANGER OF CONTAINED REVIVAL

Revival becomes dangerous and orphaned when people try to contain it. Some want to preserve the experience instead of extending the mission. It is ironic that some want to "bottle" the move of the Spirit rather than spread it. They are afraid if they spread it, they will lose it, but we know by the scriptures that whatever you sow you reap. We gain by giving. We increase by releasing. What we do not want to lose will be lost if we confine it.

We want the fire of revival to spread, and fire is spread by contact. Revival stays alive when it is allowed to flow outward.

THE POSTURE OF SERVICE

The best posture in this phase is surrender. It is here where God begins to do the unexplainable and the unpredictable, not just in you but through you. A surrendered life becomes a channel through which God reveals Himself to others.

Those who choose to serve often see facets of God's character that spectators never experience. How is this possible? They position themselves for it. Sometimes the deepest encounters with God often happen while ministering to others.

I love to hear stories and testimonies of what God did to and for a person, but what really gets me excited is hearing testimonies of what God did with and through a person. Because this is one of the highest aims and purposes of revival.

THE CYCLE CONTINUES

This is the rhythm of true revival. Not a single moment, but a lifetime of holy cycles, awakening, refining, empowering, and sending. Revival does not move in circles, leaving us where we began. It moves in cycles, each turn taking us deeper into God and farther into His purposes. Encounter leads to transformation. Transformation leads to mission. Mission leads to a deeper encounter. And so the fire continues until a people are formed who no longer merely experience revival, but carry it wherever they go.

26

DEPLOYED!

Recently, I read about a young soldier who returned from a deployment overseas. He said something I will not forget.

Before he left for combat, he spent months in training with his fellow soldiers. He learned procedures. He memorized protocols. Every day he practiced maneuvers until they became second nature. The instructors pushed him physically and mentally until he thought he could not go any farther. He said, "Training was intense. It changed me. But deep down, I knew training was not the mission."

Then the day came when his orders arrived.

His unit gathered in a large room while a commanding officer read the deployment directive. The atmosphere shifted instantly. Everyone was nervous and excited at the same time. Training had prepared them, but deployment would test them. Everything suddenly became real.

When the day came for their deployment, families cried together. Wives held their husbands tightly. Parents embraced their sons and daughters longer than usual. They comforted one another while some soldiers stood quietly, staring at the floor, absorbing the weight of what lay ahead.

Then he said something that struck deeply: "We did not train all that time just to stay on the base. Training prepared us, but deployment was the reason we existed."

He explained that a soldier who refuses deployment has misunderstood his purpose. A soldier is not trained simply to become skilled. He is trained in order to be sent.

The training, the discipline, the preparation, the hardship, all of it points toward one moment: deployment. Without deployment, training has no mission, and preparation has no purpose. Without deployment, the army never advances.

If revival only changes us but never sends us, something essential is missing. Yes, the encounter you had was real; it is undeniable. The transformation others have seen in you is proven; however, without us spreading the Good News to others, the mission of revival is incomplete. Work remains to be done.

THE DAY REVIVAL BECOMES REAL

There comes a moment when every revived believer must answer a simple question: *Will I stay here and enjoy what God has done for me, or will I go where He sends me?*

Now, let me be clear. Deployment does not mean abandoning revival. I have witnessed this. It does not mean leaving the place of power. The revival becomes your center of strength, your supply line, your home base. You cannot abandon it. You have to stay connected and remain involved.

Here is why: Soldiers deploy from a base, but they stay connected to it. The base is where they are resupplied, strengthened, and reoriented for the mission. Without the base, deployment collapses. In the same way, revival becomes the hub from which we are sent and the place to which we return for renewal and strength. Deployment is not disconnection; it is extension.

Deployment is the moment revival becomes real. It is when the prayers you prayed turn into action. This is when revival leaves the building and enters the world.

DEPLOYMENT ALWAYS COSTS SOMETHING

Every true deployment requires sacrifice. The soldier leaves home. The missionary leaves the comfort of a cozy life. The servant gives time. The intercessor loses sleep. The giver releases resources.

Deployment always costs something. I have watched this happen in the North Georgia Revival. Our people have answered the call to serve. People rearranged their schedules in order to pray. They often drive long distances to help others. They have used vacation days to serve during our conferences. They stayed late and oftentimes into the next morning, serving those who were getting baptized. They gave money they could have spent elsewhere, but they gave because God was moving. Some have missed significant family events to serve others and the Lord.

Time and time again, they have said no to comfort and convenience so they could say yes to calling. Deployment always costs something, but what it produces is eternal.

Imagine a hospital that never discharged patients. Everyone would remain in their beds responding to the nurses' commands. Doctors would continue with endless examinations. But no one would ever go home healed. Eventually, the hospital would fill beyond capacity, not because healing was absent, but because release never happened. Healing is incomplete until the patient leaves the hospital and lives again.

Revival is similar. Church services are the treatment room. God heals hearts and restores lives and renews strength. But eventually the healed must return to the world God has called them to reach.

Revival is not complete until the healed become healers.

Revival is never meant to become a reservoir. Reservoirs collect water—that is what they are made to do. But we are not to be reservoirs, we are to be rivers. Rivers release water. Reservoirs, due to a lack of movement, eventually stagnate; however, rivers stay fresh because they keep moving.

God never intended any revival to become a contained lake of blessing. Revival is meant to become a flowing river of life.

Jesus said, "*...out of his heart will flow rivers of living water*" (John 7:38 NKJV). Notice the language. Rivers! Not a pool, not a reservoir, not a lake, not a pond. *Rivers!*

Revival must flow outward, or it eventually loses its life-giving force.

I want to be clear about this issue. God has a multilayer purpose for revival, and deployment is a part of true revival. Everyone has to understand that deployment is not the loss of revival; it is actually proof that heaven sanctions what is happening in the building. In other words, what believers involved in the revival are experiencing is not only real but necessary.

One day, every believer who has experienced revival will hear the same question from God in one form or another: *What did you do with what I gave you?* The fire was never meant to stay on the altar. The power was never meant to remain in the meeting. The glory was never meant to stay in the room.

Revival prepares us, but deployment fulfills us. God does not revive people so they can remain gathered. He revives them so they can be sent. And when a revived people step into their assignment, the fire that once fell in one place begins to spread everywhere. That is deployment. That is service. And that is how revival changes the world.

PART SIX

GUARDING THE FIRE

27

WATCHING A REVIVAL'S DEATH

Let me give you an image you have probably seen before.

You are driving down a quiet country road, and in the distance, you notice a large number of birds circling in the sky. You don't need a sign or explanation. You already know what that means.

Something is dead.

Or something is dying.

Those birds are buzzards, and their presence overhead tells a story long before you reach the scene. Buzzards do not appear where life is thriving. They gather where decay has begun. They are scavengers. They don't hunt, and they don't fight for territory. Buzzards only show up after life has left.

These birds wait until something else does the stalking, the pursuit, and the kill. Then they circle, watch, and descend only when something is already dead or dying.

As an avid hunter, I have watched these birds carefully. They will perch at a distance and study the animal on the ground. They circle overhead waiting for certainty. They want to be absolutely convinced that the animal is no longer breathing. Only then do they swoop down to feed.

THE BUZZARDS ARE CIRCLING

There is a danger in the body of Christ to conduct ourselves in a similar fashion. Watching and waiting until something happens and then stepping in once the work has already been done. I do not say this to condemn anyone, but to challenge us to reconsider our posture.

There is a subtle temptation to become consumers instead of contributors, observers instead of participants. Some believers stand at a safe distance while others pray, labor, sacrifice, and contend for revival. Then, when the presence of God begins to move, they step in to enjoy the benefits.

But revival was never meant to be watched or cheered on as a fan from the sidelines. Revival is not given simply to enjoy it; revival was meant to be carried.

I want to be part of the history makers, the movers and shakers. I don't want to watch from a distance while the rest of my friends are doing the hard work and heavy lifting. I want to be in the fight, not an observer.

It is true, buzzards and lazy Christians share one defining trait—they live off what others have already produced.

REVIVAL DOES NOT SURVIVE SCAVENGERS

Revival is not sustained by spectators. It is stewarded by servants. Moves of God never die on their own. What happens? The ones responsible for stewarding the move of God simply get tired, distracted, and or overwhelmed and stop contending for His presence. Revivals fade when participants become observers and when the warriors become consumers.

When a person gets to this point in the cycles of their walk with God and chooses to slow down, pull out, or no longer remain active, a slow drift occurs. Things will begin to fade in their spiritual life. First, they will stop feverishly pursuing God. Second, contending for personal holiness will lessen, and third, the pull and necessity for laboring in corporate and private prayer will grind to a halt. Prayer becomes less important. Worship becomes routine instead of exciting and alive. Scripture reading becomes occasional instead of essential. Compromise that once grieved the heart becomes tolerable.

These observations are not theories or pastoral rhetoric; each is a reality. I have seen this with my own eyes. Words such as discipline, repentance, time, sacrifice, and obedience become offensive and no longer appealing. Why, because revival demands something that you are no longer willing to give. Yet, we feed off another person's sacrifice, labor, prayer life, and acts of service. We thankfully partake of the harvest, but have neglected the plowing, planting, and watering.

You move into a reality where you survive and at times even thrive on leftover revelation, borrowed fire, and secondhand encounters. You scavenge.

Just existing is boring.

Going through the motions is mundane and emotionally exhausting, not to mention consistently uneventful. God placed something inside you that longs for adventure. It is there and you may never have tapped into it, but you are about to. We are to be far more dangerous than we actually are. You were made for engagement.

Before I share with you how to step into that adventurous walk with God, let me ask you a question: "What threat level are you to the kingdom of darkness?" I am not asking you how long you have been in Church or what level of education you have, or what title you carry. In fact, I am not even asking how many followers you have on social media or how many gifts of the Spirit you operate in.

Rather, I am asking what danger do you genuinely pose to the work of the enemy? Just for the record, hell is not intimidated by information, shaken by our attendance at church or conferences, nor is he threatened by our ministry activity. However, he is concerned when a believer begins to not only talk about revival, visit revival, serve in the revival, but to carry revival.

THERE IS A LION INSIDE YOU

Regardless of your current standing in life, level of surrender, and engagement in the work of the Lord, I want you to realize there is a lion within you. Revelation 5:5 calls Jesus *"the Lion of the tribe of Judah,"* and that Lion lives within every believer. This is not theoretical; it is practical—He lives in you. His nature is in you. As a result, we are true sons and daughters of His; therefore, His DNA is in us. Look, you and I were designed to live strong, bold lives. We were created to move with authority, purpose, and strength.

Lions do not scavenge; they hunt, advance, and take territory. When a lion enters a region or new territory, all other animals know it. Predators move with intention. Being a scavenger is not in our spiritual code; it is something we have to learn to do. In the kingdom of God, we are called to be the predator, not the prey. The lion within you is about to be released from its cage!

As I have witnessed in nature, prey live in constant reaction mode while predators move with intention. Prey is driven by fear and seeks to survive. They hide. They are constantly on the lookout for possible danger. They are vulnerable and are targets. However, predators are driven by purpose and seek to take and protect their territory and to gain new ground.

When believers tap the brakes on their advancement and pursuit of Christ, decline begins. Not immediately, but inevitably, passion fades, and they lose their fire. Their survival depends entirely on leftovers, decay, and what others have abandoned.

My fear is that too many will simply rely on the hard efforts of others and become spiritual scavengers. This is tragic for all involved. I have learned a sobering truth—revival is not sustained by spectators, it is stewarded by servants.

Revival comes to awaken lions, not simply to feed buzzards; therefore, God is calling you out of observation and into engagement.

28

"WHATEVER YOU DO, DON'T LET IT GO!"

I carry a fear that refuses to leave me. Not the kind of fear that paralyzes, but the kind that protects. The kind of fear you feel when holding something fragile and irreplaceable. The kind of fear that whispers, *Be careful. What you are holding matters.* That is the fear I feel about the move of God we are experiencing at Christ Fellowship Church.

Some people will quickly tell me that I should not be afraid. Their concern is well-intended, but only partially true, because not all fear is bad. In fact, some fear is healthy.

When a person stands at the edge of a cliff and looks down 100 feet to the rocks below, fear rushes in. That fear is not destructive; it is protective. It is a gift that keeps us from stepping too close to the edge. In the same way, a healthy fear of financial instability can keep a person from reckless spending and irresponsible decisions.

Not all fear is harmful. Some fears are gifts from God, placed within us to guard what matters most. Healthy fear does not drive us away from God; it draws us closer while teaching us what must be protected.

My aim is to help us learn how to protect what God has entrusted to us, our spiritual growth, our calling, and the moves of God we pray so desperately to see.

TWO TYPES OF FEAR

Destructive fear pushes you away from God, whereas protective fear draws you closer to Him. One produces anxiety, trepidation, and instability; the other produces vigilance and inspires responsibility.

Scripture also teaches us to have a healthy fear of sin. Sin has the power to enslave and destroy, and the enemy constantly sets traps designed to lure us back into old patterns. A healthy fear of sin becomes a guardrail that protects our freedom and maintains our testimony before people.

One thing I have learned about healthy fear is that it can keep you safe and focused. What do I mean? Well, in some cases, whenever we lose our fear of someone or something, we can get careless and presumptuous. This can lead to mishandling what has been entrusted to us.

The Hebrides Revival broke out in 1949 on the Isle of Lewis, Scotland, and became one of the most remarkable moves of God in the 20th century. Two sisters, Peggy and Christine Smith, 84 and 82, began to pray fervently for God to move among the people, especially among the young people. Their consistent commitment to prayer, along with the others who joined them, created an opportunity for God to come down on their island.

In late 1949, God moved powerfully in a barn in Barvas, Scotland. That initial spark changed an entire region. A supernatural awareness of God fell upon people everywhere. Men and women, young and old, religious and nonreligious people were shaken to their core with the fear of God as people were convicted over their sin. People feared dying in their sin and being eternally separated from God; they would weep and cry out without dignity, "Is there mercy for me?"

God moved in the churches, dance halls, schools, jailhouses, and even in the open fields. Many would fall to the ground begging for salvation even before they reached the church house. They would lie on the ground and weep. Some clutched fence posts because they could not walk another step without repenting and securing their peace with God.

Duncan Campbell became the primary evangelist of the Hebrides Revival; however, he did not ignite it. He simply stepped into a move of God that had already begun before he set foot on the island.

According to reports, some meetings consistently lasted until 4 a.m., only to begin again the next day. People were so desperate for an encounter with God that many refused to leave the presence of God. People were not drawn to come hear a famous preacher or high-profile personality; no, they were drawn to the glory of God.

In 1968, in a sermon, Duncan Campbell said regarding the revival, "An awareness of God gripped the whole community."[40] In some villages, the weight of God was so intense that nearly entire communities were born again within days. God's work was precise and quick. God seemed to be everywhere; they could not escape His fiery conviction. People would stop on the side of the road and get on their knees, crying out to God. There was no misunderstanding that God was at work. God had settled over the islands.

For nearly three years, the revival spread from island to island and from village to village. Everywhere, people were saying the same thing: "God came down."

Some unusual manifestations occurred. A dance hall miles away from the closest church suddenly emptied because the young people fell under conviction of their sin and rebellion against God. Campbell said God struck the hall "like a lightning flash from heaven."

In addition, people would leave the revival service early in the morning and return home around 5 a.m. and have to be at work at 7 a.m. The report was that people would not get tired. This phenomenon was supernatural, and God graced the people during this time: lights would appear to show people the way home in the dark, and a home was shaken as if from an earthquake (dishes and silverware falling off the table) while people were praying and worshiping.[41]

How did this incredible revival end? This is a great question. Even though a move of God never ends on one thing alone, there are factors that cause revivals to decline and eventually dissipate.

Years after the Hebrides Revival, Duncan Campbell tells the story of a journalist who traveled to where the revival began. His aim was to take a deep dive into the revival and figure out how it began, and to research the long-lasting effects of the move of God.

Campbell said, "And as he finished up, amazingly, he booked into the guest house, which was run by an elderly couple. And the guy who was the father of the house was actually one of the fathers of the revival. And so (the journalist) found himself, without trying, sitting right at the feet of someone who could tell him a lot of information."

With tears in his eyes, this guy said to him, "You know, there are six of us who were like the fathers of the revival who are still alive. We meet together occasionally when our wives are in bed. We sit down, and we talk about those days. We can't stop crying." And he said, "The reason that the Hebridean Revival faded was because the leadership didn't know what to do with it. They did not know how to structure it. They did not know how to prepare a wineskin for what God was doing, and it faulted, and it failed."

Campbell continues, "And this old man got ahold of my friend who is probably about thirty years of age, grabbed him by the collar looked at him in his eyes. His piercing eyes looking at him and said, 'SON, WHEN YOU GET IT, WHATEVER YOU DO, DO NOT LET GO OF IT!'"

This is it! What a declaration. In fact, those words will not leave me alone.

Tragically, over time how many people have "let go" what God birthed? I have witnessed this far too many times. They constantly echo in my head. This is a sobering reminder spoken by an eyewitness of one of the greatest moves of God our world has ever seen.

GUARD WHAT YOU HAVE WORKED FOR

The apostle John said something similar in 2 John 1:8 (NLT), "*Watch out that you do not lose what we have worked so hard to achieve. Be diligent so that you receive your full reward.*"

Your spiritual growth and perhaps the revival you are experiencing did not happen simply because God decided to sovereignly send revival to a particular location. It came because people worked at creating the correct culture that God would be attracted to. The people prayed, became broken, sought His face, and repented of their sin. The result? The presence of God filled our lives, homes, and our church. God's glory came.

Did you know that even after all the hard work, endless hours of prayer, and serving others, it is possible for the Lord to lift His manifest presence? However, the glory will not cease because God desires for it to lift; no, it will lift when we "let go of it." John warned us, "Do not lose what you worked hard to attain. Do not let it slip through your fingers." The consequences are at least twofold. One, we will forfeit all that could have been if we had just continued to guard and sustain the move of God. Second, we will fail to receive the *"full reward."*

If we retreat or cease to cooperate with the work of God, we will receive a reward for our labor up to the point when we let go of the work. However, we will not receive the full reward we could have received if we had remained faithful and held on.

Let me give you an example of this from the marketplace. Let's say I buy 100 shares of stock from a start-up company at $3.00 per share. I have a $300.00 investment in the new company. After one year, I decide to sell my 100 shares. Now the shares are $4.00 a share. I receive the benefits of my investment, which would be a total of $100 plus my $300 initial investment. Now I have $400. I received my reward.

Now, let's say that during the next year, the company exponentially grows and its stock price reaches $20.00 per share. Because I sold my shares at $4.00 per share, I am not entitled to reap the benefits of the successful company.

The apostle John warned us, "Hey, you guys worked too hard to let go of what you labored for, and if you do let go, you will not receive the full reward."

Let me encourage you—do not pull back. Do not take a break, do not withdraw from your walk with God, nor your labor of love in the kingdom of God. You have sacrificed too much to forfeit the future dividends—both on earth and in heaven.

Will this revival come to an end? Not sure. Perhaps. Maybe. I hope it does not. A lot depends on how me, our leaders, and our church navigates through the seasons. We get to determine how much glory we are willing to carry and how long we will carry it.

The mandate from the old man is clear, "WHATEVER YOU DO…DON'T LET IT GO!"

29

CODE RED!

I recently heard someone say, "We went from green to Code Red without even passing yellow."

Code Red is never called because something might go wrong. It is called because something is already going wrong.

"Code Red" is a universal signal of danger. It means a serious threat is present, and normal operations must stop, and immediate action is required. No delay. No distraction. No excuses.

In the military, Code Red is issued during active combat or when an imminent threat is detected.

Hospitals call Code Red when there is a fire, a violent incident, or an immediate life-threatening emergency.

Law enforcement declares a Code Red when an active shooter or extreme danger is present.

Industries sound Code Red when there is a catastrophic system failure.

I must say it again, Code Red requires an instant response. In other words, "Drop everything. This cannot wait." Code Red is the highest level of urgency, a warning that what is at stake cannot survive delay, distraction, or disobedience.

HEAVEN SOUNDS THE ALARM

I believe we are living in a Code Red moment—in our world, culture, in our families, and even in our churches. The world is on fire.

There are moments when heaven sounds the alarm. Not with sirens, not with flashing lights, but a subtle withdrawal of weight. Or a whisper from the Holy Spirit, *"Something is wrong!"*

History is filled with movements that once shook cities and now barely whisper or breathe at all. Not because God stopped moving, but because someone missed the Code Red moment. Every awakening eventually reaches a fragile stage. And the longer a move of God exists, the more fragile moments will surface.

Every move of God birthed in revival fire reaches a point where it must be tended to, or it will thin and die. Code Red is about recognition. It is about measurement. And the future of what God does next often depends on whether someone has the courage to say, "Something has shifted, and we must respond."

WHEN THE WEIGHT CHANGES

There have been moments during the North Georgia Revival when I walked into the sanctuary, and something felt off. Yes, the room was full of people, the worship was strong, the band was on cue, the crowd was engaged, and everything looked right. However, something was not right; it was subtle, almost imperceptible. Something had shifted. The atmosphere felt lighter. The weight was different. The glory felt thinner.

There was a room full of people who did not realize the Holy Spirit had been grieved, but I knew.

I don't know if you have ever experienced that, but it concerns me when I do. My mind shifts into, "What's wrong?" And, "How do I fix it?"

There are many reasons why this happens during moves of God and even in our personal lives. It could be quiet tension among the key leaders. A disagreement among staff members that went unresolved. Or, someone could have had their feelings hurt and felt overlooked. There are other things that could lead to this vacuum, including pride, inconsistencies, entitlement, and familiarity.

Moments like these do occur. No revival or move of God is perfect. In my situation, it wasn't that God departed; He simply pulled back. I could feel it. He was like a wounded friend who grows quiet at the table, or a spouse who quietly retreats after being bruised by their spouse's words.

When this happens it is a Code Red moment. Yes, everything externally looks the same, sounds the same, but the weight of heaven in the room has changed. God has not left the room, but the atmosphere has shifted. In actuality, the glory has thinned. At this point, we cannot pretend everything is normal, for it is not. Ignoring what God has highlighted can have eternal consequences. And turning up the music will not fix it. Preaching louder will not fix it. Marketing will not fix it. You cannot manufacture God's weight; something has to be corrected.

I have learned the hard way that when heaven sounds the alarm, it is not a suggestion; it is a summons. Someone has to address the issues at hand. It is not a moment of panic; however, urgency is a necessity. Wisdom, authentic humility, and repentance are required at this point. If the issue(s) are not dealt with, the revival will not end suddenly or in a few days, and it may even continue for weeks, but the heavy presence of God will slowly lift. If unattended, God will withdraw and become silent, and the glory will fade. then we are left with nothing but activity, songs, words, and no power.

Someone has to guard the glory, protect the room. Someone has to defend the atmosphere. Someone has to guard the awe. This is an enormous responsibility and can be overwhelming at times.

THE COST OF IGNORING

In natural emergencies, ignoring Code Red costs lives. When time is of the essence, a response is needed. When life is dangling in the balance, seconds matter. In spiritual realities, time matters as well, and ignoring heaven's alarm may not cost lives, but it does cost presence.

This is not a call to fear, but a call to awareness. It is a summons to guard what heaven has given. Because God wants revivals and moves of His Spirit to continue, He will call a Code Red. In this moment, God searches the room for someone awake enough to notice. Someone humble enough to respond. Someone bold enough to call it what it is. What is at stake is not attendance, influence, or reputation—it is presence. And presence, once withdrawn, does not return cheaply.

30

BE CAREFUL HOW WE TREAT THE HOLY SPIRIT

I once heard a pastor describe revival this way: "When God visits a people, it is like a king entering the room." Everyone immediately senses the change in atmosphere. Conversations quiet. Attention shifts. The moment becomes sacred. When a king is present, how people conduct themselves matters.

Revival is the same way.

When the Holy Spirit draws near to a people, heaven has entrusted them with something priceless. How they treat His presence determines whether the visitation deepens—or fades.

This is why revival history repeatedly shows that the greatest threat to a move of God is not persecution from the outside, but carelessness from within.

These careless assaults on a move of God are real and can ruin any move of the Holy Spirit. It was Charles Finney who said these sobering words, "The Spirit of God is grieved away by sin, neglect of prayer, and by lightness in divine things. Revival never survives such treatment." Please do not read past Finney's words too quickly. They carry kindgom significance. The last phrase is provoking and sobering: "...revival never survives such treatment."[42]

In other words, revival is not destroyed primarily by outside opposition. It most often fades because of how God's own people treat His presence.

How are we treating the Holy Spirit? What are we doing to please Him, honor Him, esteem Him, yield to Him? He is our aim, not the results of revival, not the manifestations, not the fruit. It is Him. We must pursue and love Him without distraction.

STRONG LEADERSHIP IS NECESSARY

In the North Georgia Revival, there have been times when we had to be both proactive and responsive to issues. Some of our decisions were not popular, and any of the issues left unaddressed had the potential to halt what God was doing in our midst.

Our leadership team has remained singularly focused on one enduring mission: to fiercely guard the presence of God and ensure that He never leaves us. We understood early that revival is not merely something you host—it is something you must protect.

One day after concluding that what we were experiencing at Christ Fellowship Church was a genuine move of God. I asked God, "God, how do I pastor this move of Your Spirit?" I heard Him clearly, and I still hear it today. He said, "Hold it loosely and guard it ferociously."

I recently heard a college football coach discuss the price of leadership. He said something that stuck with me: leadership always has a cost, and the greatest leaders are simply those who are willing to bear it. He listed the cost of strong leadership: (1) You will have to make hard decisions that negatively affect people you care about. (2) You will be disliked despite your best attempt to do the best for the most. (3) You will be misunderstood and will not always have the opportunity to defend yourself.

I believe this is especially true when leading during a move of God. Revival leadership carries a unique weight because the decisions being made are not merely organizational; they are spiritual. When God begins to move, leaders must guard the atmosphere, protect unity, and make difficult choices that preserve what heaven has entrusted to them. At times, that means slowing things down when others want to accelerate, correcting behavior that threatens the purity of the movement, or choosing long-term health over short-term excitement.

These decisions are rarely celebrated in the moment, but they are necessary if revival is to mature and endure. Throughout the cycles of revival, leadership becomes one of the primary ways God protects what He has birthed. Without leaders willing to bear the cost, what began in power can easily collapse under the weight of immaturity.

Dr. Michael Brown, who led the Brownsville Revival School of Ministry and served as a key leader in the outpouring in Pensacola, Florida, warned that revival fires are fragile and must be stewarded with humility, holiness, discernment, and balance.[43] He added, "Every genuine revival faces dangers, excess, imbalance, pride, and division. If not addressed, these can diminish the impact of what God is doing."[44]

Duncan Campbell, leader of the Hebrides Revival, often noted that the Spirit's manifest presence would lift whenever pride, disunity, or hidden sin was present. He recounted several occasions where revival "was hindered until sin was brought into the light," and only after confession did "the power of God fall again."[45]

Campbell remarked that revival is not sustained by meetings, preaching, or even miracles; it is sustained by the purity of the vessels hosting the presence of God.

Something important must be understood here. The Spirit of God is not grieved because His kingdom is threatened; He is grieved because the relationship with His people has been wounded.

A.W. Tozer said, "The Holy Spirit is a gentle dove, not a predatory bird. When we ignore Him, resist Him, or insult Him, He quietly withdraws and leaves us to our own devices."[46]

The Spirit of God does not compete for attention. When He is dishonored, He simply becomes quiet.

If revival history has taught us anything, it has taught us this: The Holy Spirit is not driven away by our weakness, but by our resistance. Not by our brokenness, but by our pride; not by our need, but by our neglect. It has also taught us that revival begins to fade when people stop valuing what birthed the revival.

I don't mean to oversimplify matters, but the truth remains: What started the revival is what sustains revival. Any shift from the core ingredients dooms the move of God to a premature ending.

If prayer births revival, and it does, then prayer must sustain it. If humility contributes to the beginning of revival, and it does, the humility must remain to sustain it. If brokenness birthed the move of God, and it does, then a broken spirit before the Lord must remain to sustain it.

When the ingredients that birthed revival disappear, the atmosphere that carried revival begins to thin.

THE POWER OF NEGLECT

It does not take a scandal or moral collapse to weaken the weight of God in a church or revival. Sometimes it happens through something far more subtle. Neglect. Subtle neglect.

Have you ever noticed how homes that are lived in seem to last longer and look better than homes that sit vacant? Vacant homes slowly deteriorate. The house literally falls apart. The house was built to have activity, to respond to use, to movement, to laughter, to the rhythms of life. When neglected mechanical systems fail, seals crack, and motors seize. It is as if the house forgets how to function—it needs presence.

This phenomenon is well documented not only by construction engineers but also by property managers, insurance companies, and building scientists.

A nationally referenced real estate analysis discovered that vacant houses tend to take longer to sell and often sell for significantly less than occupied homes. On average, vacant houses sold for approximately $11,000 less than comparable occupied homes.[47]

But the real problem is not just financial, it is structural.

One of the main reasons occupied homes last longer and look healthier is the activity that keeps the environment stable. Heating and cooling systems operate regularly. Doors open and close, therefore, allowing air to circulate.

In vacant houses, humidity rises and lingers, allowing condensation to build. The end result, mold begins to grow and thrive. Rot begins to spread. And rot does not need permission to do its work; it only needs absence. Then come the invaders. Rodents. Termites.

Birds. Bats. Squirrels. Pests are free to roam at their leisure. Without footsteps, noise, or human movement, they nest, they eat, they multiply, and destroy. Many know from experience how much damage these small creatures can cause. It can be exponential.

The bottom line is simple—a house deteriorates faster when not lived in because presence equals stewardship. Houses need presence to thrive.

The same is true spiritually. The enemy watches. And he understands something many believers overlook. He does not need to destroy what believers neglect. In time, the neglect will accomplish the enemy's overall objective.

Spiritual decline rarely begins with an outright attack; it begins with neglect. When vision fades, discipline loosens. When prayer weakens, when personal Bible study is "hit or miss," or passion cools, decay quietly sets in. It fills the void.

The weakening of the presence of God in our lives, churches, and ministries often begins when neglect is allowed to linger.

What was once thriving and vibrant slowly suffocates. As one presence leaves the house, another takes its place. An eerie stillness fills the rooms. You can sense it. Most people who walk through houses while looking to buy understand this. They can immediately sense the difference between a house that has been lived in recently and one that has been empty for months.

Realtors know that occupied homes sell faster than vacant ones. Why? Because presence communicates life.

Revival atmospheres function the same way. The presence of God rests where hearts remain attentive, hungry, and responsive. But when vigilance fades, and attention drifts, the atmosphere changes.

Not suddenly, but gradually.

More often our personal fire fades the same way vacant houses decay, through the slow withdrawal of attention from what matters most.

Vigilance is a necessity if you are to maintain intimacy with the Holy Spirit. Because revival is not sustained by one great encounter with God, it is sustained by thousands of daily decisions that say: "Your presence matters more than anything else."

31

GRIEVING THE SPIRIT

The Bible speaks of two distinct but related dangers in our relationship with the Holy Spirit: grieving Him and quenching Him. Although some treat these two actions as the same, revival history clearly demonstrates they are not identical.

Continually grieving the Spirit wounds intimacy and can cause revival to fade because the heart of the Father is wounded. Quenching the Spirit, on the other hand, can end a move of God by attempting to restrain or control what God is doing. One damages the relationship; the other restricts the expression. One wounds the heart of the Spirit; the other suppresses the activity of the Spirit. Both are dangerous. Both can darken revival.

Let's take an in-depth look at these two behaviors so we can avoid disrupting the work of God.

The subject of *grieving the Holy Spirit* is one of the most spiritually weighty themes in all of the Bible. Yet it is strangely absent in much modern preaching. According to Ephesians 4:30 (NKJV), the apostle Paul gives a direct warning: *"Do not grieve the Holy Spirit of God, by whom you were sealed for the day of redemption."*

Because Paul addressed this issue so plainly, we must take it seriously. If the Spirit of God can be grieved, then the people of God must learn how to guard His presence.

As the Bible unfolds, the ministry and personality of the Holy Spirit are clearly revealed. The Holy Spirit is not an impersonal force; He is a divine Person who relates to us personally. Scripture shows us that the Holy Spirit:

- Speaks and testifies and inspires (Mark 13:11, Acts 2:4)
- Can be sinned against (Matthew 12:31)
- Can be lied to (Acts 5:3)
- Can be tested, tempted (Acts 5:9)
- Can even be insulted (Hebrews 10:29)

In addition, He strengthens (Ephesians 3:16), teaches (Luke 12:12, John 14:26, 1 Corinthians 2:13), and encourages believers (Acts 9:31).

Therefore, He can be grieved. The fact that the Holy Spirit can be grieved tells us something profound—our relationship with Him is deeply personal, not mechanical or frigid, but fluid.

I sometimes wonder why we hear so little about this high-stakes subject. It just may be me, but it seems that our pulpits focus more on helping people discover their identity, fulfill their dreams, or pursue their destiny than they do on asking the deeper questions that shape our relationship with God.

Questions such as:

- What draws the Holy Spirit closer to us?
- What causes Him to withdraw?
- How does the Holy Spirit feel about my current spiritual condition?
- What actions am I taking that wound the Holy Spirit?
- What causes His presence to lift from my life and church?

These are probing questions that should be asked frequently, both individually and corporately. It is true that revival has the opportunity to thrive where these questions are taken seriously.

Let's begin with a foundational understanding that it is possible for a son or daughter of God to offend the person of the Holy Spirit.

We all understand what it feels like to be grieved by someone close to us. This happens when a friend or loved one does something that wounds the relationship. The closeness that once existed suddenly feels strained.

The Holy Spirit loves us, and He, too, can be grieved. And one of the ways we grieve Him is when our love for Jesus gets diverted. When the flame of our affection begins to burn for something else—for example, ambition, recognition, comfort, or distraction—the closeness of our relationship with Him begins to fracture.

All too well, I know what begins as a small distraction can slowly grow into a divided heart.

The Bible gives us multiple examples of individuals and even entire nations grieving the Spirit of God:

- David grieved the Lord through his sin with Bathsheba (2 Samuel 11).
- Saul grieved God through disobedience when he spared King Agag (1 Samuel 15).
- Samson betrayed his assignment on the lap of Delilah (Judges 16:19).
- Moses struck the rock in frustration rather than honoring God before the people (Numbers 20:7-12).
- Ananias and Sapphira lied to the Holy Spirit in the early Church (Acts 5:1-11).

To grieve someone does not necessarily end the relationship, but it wounds the heart of the one who loves you. And when a heart is wounded, the natural response is often a quiet *pulling back,* not abandonment. Influential Welsh minister and medical doctor Martyn Lloyd-Jones explained that grieving the Holy Spirit is to disappoint Him when you don't listen to His promptings that come to your heart and mind.[48]

The Spirit does not usually depart suddenly. More often He grows quiet when His voice is repeatedly ignored. When the Spirit is grieved, heaven pauses and waits.

Consider a simple illustration.

Imagine a husband and wife who have been married for many years and deeply love one another. There is no doubt that their relationship is secure, covenantal, and committed. In fact, never once have they even thought of or discussed divorce. But one day, the husband dismisses something that deeply matters to his wife, perhaps her feelings, her boundaries, or her words. She becomes hurt and grieved. Over the next few hours, he notices something has changed. She becomes unusually quiet and withdrawn. She has not stopped loving him, but the nearness they once enjoyed feels strained. She has not withdrawn to punish him. Her heart is simply wounded. The relationship still exists, but the closeness has been affected.

That is what grieving the Holy Spirit looks like. Not the loss of relationship, but the loss of closeness. Nearness.

Grief is a relational language; it assumes closeness. This is why the nearness of God must be treasured. Revival lives or dies on the value people place on the nearness of God. However, I am afraid not everyone does. Leonard Ravenhill said it best: "The greatest tragedy is that the presence of God is not in the church, and nobody misses Him."[49] His statement is epic: "…the presence of God is not in the church, and nobody misses Him." This should send shock waves through our souls.

Is it even possible to miss God's presence? To not even recognize that He is not among us? I believe so.

Paul's instruction in Ephesians 4:30 carries another powerful insight. In the Greek text, the command is written in the present tense, meaning it is an ongoing command. In other words, believers are continually commanded not to grieve the Holy Spirit. This is not the language of legalism but the language of love. I have drawn the conclusion that love is observable. You notice it. True love becomes careful, because it never wants to wound the heart of the one it loves. So, every day, every decision, every attitude, every response should be closely monitored.

When people truly value the presence of God, they begin to guard their lives carefully. They guard their attitudes. They guard their words. They guard their relationships. They guard their obedience. Because they understand something many people forget—intimacy with our beautiful Savior is not automatic. It is a gift and should be treasured.

And every person must decide whether they will treat that gift casually or treasure it deeply enough to protect it.

32

WHEN THE SPIRIT OF GOD CANNOT BREATHE

The Bible is emphatic about not quenching the Spirit: *"Do not quench the Spirit. Do not despise prophecies. Test all things; hold fast what is good"* (1 Thessalonians 5:19-21 NKJV).

We have examined what it means to *grieve* the Holy Spirit. But grieving the Spirit, if left unresolved, rarely remains isolated. What begins as grief can eventually lead to something far more serious, *quenching* the Spirit.

Grieving wounds the relationship. Quenching suppresses the activity. In many cases, quenching the Spirit is simply the end result of repeatedly ignoring the Spirit's grief.

Let's think about this. Is it even possible for humans, God's created beings, to possess the power to restrict the moving of the Holy Spirit? According to the apostle Paul, the answer is an emphatic, yes.

In God's governmental plan of earth, God has given us human agents incredible authority; authority that can cooperate with the Spirit or resist Him.

That authority includes the sobering ability to stifle, squelch, limit, or even stop the active working of the Holy Spirit in a given place. Frank Bartleman noted, "The Spirit will not be managed. Attempts to control Him always end in His withdrawal."[50]

WHAT IT MEANS TO QUENCH THE SPIRIT

I want to ask two questions: (1) What does it really mean to quench the Spirit of God? And the one question I think we all want answered: (2) How does it happen?

- Quenching the Spirit is almost never the result of a single moment. It is usually the final stage of a longer spiritual process. That process often begins with grieving the Spirit.
- Quenching the Spirit of God is a suffocation, smothering; it is likened to choking life out of something. Another word picture is putting water on a fire to put out the flame.
- Quenching the Holy Spirit is more than resisting Him; it is more aggressive than that.

Here is what I believe happens on the road to quenching the Holy Spirit.

The Spirit convicts us of something. The Holy Spirit is warning us that something is not right and needs to be addressed and corrected. When those promptings are postponed, ignored, resisted, or overridden, the activity of the Spirit becomes suppressed. Quenching the Spirit is simply grieving Him long enough that His activity becomes restrained.

Revival historians often use the image of a river to explain how the Spirit's work becomes quenched. Imagine a powerful river flowing freely down from the mountains. The current is strong, life-giving, and unstoppable. Entire communities downstream depend on that river for life.

Now imagine someone slowly building a dam across that river. At first, the change is almost unnoticeable. The river still flows, the water still moves, and life continues as usual. But as more stones are added, the current weakens. The flow slows. Eventually, the water that once rushed freely is reduced to a trickle.

No one stopped the river in a single moment.

It was blocked little by little.

The same thing happens when the Holy Spirit is quenched. The Spirit still moves. Conviction still comes. Promptings are still felt. But when those promptings are ignored, resisted, or delayed, small stones begin to accumulate in the river of God's activity. Over time, the flow that once moved freely becomes restrained. What began as grieving the Spirit eventually results in quenching Him.

Revival rarely ends because God stopped moving—it ends because the river of His work was slowly obstructed. That is quenching the Holy Spirit.

Quenching the Spirit of God is like suffocating something that was once alive. As I stated previously, it is like smothering or choking the life out of something. *Grieving the Spirit is like wounding the flame, and quenching the Spirit is like extinguishing it.*

Let me be clear, to quench the Spirit does not mean we lose Him entirely, but it does mean the fire that once burned freely is no longer active in the same way.

The Greek word for *quench* is *sbennymi,* which means to "extinguish, put out a fire, to allow things to go out, to suppress, stifle." Fires rarely die instantly. They die because they are denied what sustains them.

Each of these is a concerted effort that takes time and energy to carry out. The aim is to stop something from continuing or advancing. Let me be clear, quenching the Holy Spirit rarely happens accidentally. It is usually the result of repeated choices to ignore the Spirit's conviction.

Some people may not think they are working against God. Some even believe they are protecting the church from excess or disorder. But the reality remains, actions are being taken that limit the working of the Holy Spirit.

The Azusa Street Revival (1906-1909) was a move of God that paved the way for the Pentecostal movement to spread worldwide. Even today, we still feel the global impact of what happened there. However, the movement eventually faded. Frank Bartleman, an eyewitness and chronicler of the Azusa Street revival, wrote, "We had power. But we lost the glory. Organization came in, and the Spirit went out."[51]

This statement is extremely important. Bartleman was not a critic looking from the outside. He was inside the revival. And he did not blame persecution. He did not blame the absence of hunger. He blamed man's attempt to control what God had birthed.

This is the subtle shift that often quenches revival.

At the beginning, everyone depends completely on God. But over time, people begin to trust systems, structures, and human wisdom more than the Spirit. Fervor and passion give way to skills, human strategy, and management. And when that shift happens, the Spirit is gradually pushed to the margins—not completely ignored, but not completely trusted.

I have discovered through my extensive reading on revival history that nearly every revival faded not because God arbitrarily withdrew, but because human stewardship took over the role exclusively dedicated to the Holy Spirit. People began trying to control what was meant to be surrendered.

Too often we assume God needs our perspective, our systems, our safeguards, our wisdom, and our control mechanisms. But revival does not advance through our schemes and control; it advances through dependence. Revivals continue the same way they started—an utter dependence on God and God alone. When people move from faith to fear, revival begins to weaken.

It should be noted that the most devastating moment in a people's existence is when the glory of God—His weight, His favor, His intimate interaction—with His people is lifted.

CONSEQUENCES

There are real consequences to rejecting the work of the Holy Spirit. First, it affects our personal walk with God. It places a ceiling on our spiritual growth, and it limits our maturity. In addition, it neutralizes the faith necessary to release kingdom power. In effect, we restrict the very work of God we once prayed for.

Second, it affects others. We actually limit and possibly forfeit future activity of the Holy Spirit in our lives. When the Spirit's work is quenched in our lives, people around us lose access to what God intended to release through us. It blocks God's power from reaching others who could and would have benefited from the fruit and flow of power in and through you.

33

GOD IS JEALOUS

Exodus 20:5 (NIV) — *"You shall not bow down to them or worship them; for I, the Lord your God, am a jealous God, visiting the iniquity of the fathers on the children to the third and the fourth generation of those who hate me."*

Exodus 34:14 (NKJV) — *"For you shall worship no other god, for the Lord, whose name is Jealous, is a jealous God."*

The Hebrew word translated *jealous* when describing God in the Bible is *qanna (קַנָּא)*. This word does not describe petty jealousy or emotional insecurity. It describes a fierce, covenantal passion that refuses to share what rightfully belongs to Him.

The word *jealous* is rich in its meaning. It communicates that God is zealous or intensely passionate for exclusive loyalty. It is not selfish envy but a righteous, protective fervor for His people against idolatry,

In Exodus 34:14, God even attaches this attribute to His own name: *El Qanna*, "The Jealous God."

Each name of the Lord reveals a distinct part of His nature. When God reveals Himself as El Qanna, He is declaring something unmistakable: He will not tolerate divided loyalty. The first commandment establishes this clearly: *"You shall have no other gods before Me"* (Exodus 20:3 NKJV).

God is not competing for first place among many loves; He demands the throne.

Francis Chan wrote in his book *Crazy Love:* "When God calls Himself jealous, He is saying that He refuses to share our affection with false gods."[52]

We must quickly realize something important. Experiencing God's grace does not remove His jealousy. It intensifies it. Because grace establishes a deeper relationship.

A.W. Tozer said it plainly, "God will not suffer a rival. He will not share His throne with another."[53] God wants exclusivity. Before we think this is over the top and too demanding, we must remember something essential. Christ purchased us. *"For you were bought at a price"* (1 Corinthians 6:20 NKJV). We belong to Him.

Let us be over-the-top clear. God's jealousy stems not from insecurity or emotional instability. It arises from perfect love. His jealousy is the fierce love of the Father who refuses to surrender His children to what will destroy them. He knows that sin, idols, possessions, and worldly pursuits cannot love us back. They promise fulfillment, but they produce bondage.

One of the primary causes of God's jealousy is our attraction and infatuation with sin. We cling to it and have developed a taste for it. We flirt with it. And sometimes we defend it. Duncan Campbell, speaking from firsthand revival experience, cautioned that "God is not prepared to pour out His Spirit where sin is being tolerated."[54] This is why the sanctification process is crucial in a believer's journey with the Lord.

Sin and refusal to alienate ourselves from it are often what prevent us from progressing in our relationship with God. It limits us and disrupts God's power and kingdom purposes for us.

Theologian and revivalist Andrew Murray wrote, "Every act of disobedience, every refusal to surrender, grieves the Holy Spirit and hinders His work of forming Christ within us."[55]

John Owen, English Puritan pastor, similarly warned, "There is nothing the Holy Spirit more deeply resents in us than sin—especially those sins that resist His sanctifying work."[56]

It would serve us well to remember something sobering. Revival does not end when sinners resist God; it ends when saints divide their hearts and fall in love with other things.

WHEN GOD SOUNDS THE ALARM

At the North Georgia Revival, I have discovered that sometimes God sounds an alarm. Not a whisper, but a shout. The Spirit does not simply nudge; He interrupts. "Hey, I need you to address this issue…or I need you to correct this…." "Return to Me…let that go."

When this happens, action must be taken immediately because delay can cause damage, and in some cases, irreparable damage. Delay is a brutal, silent enemy of revival.

Recently, I experienced such a moment. Something wasn't right at the North Georgia Revival. No one else seemed to notice, but I felt it in my gut. The miracles were still happening in the water. The room still carried the presence of God. The preaching was strong; the worship was excellent. Our altar calls were powerful, and there was still fire on the baptismal waters.

But when I walked into the sanctuary, something felt off; there was an uncomfortable agitation in my spirit. I didn't know what it was, but I definitely felt that the Lord was slightly grieved and unhappy about something. I didn't feel any condemnation or shame, but I knew God wanted to have a conversation with me about it.

Over the years, I have learned that long before the Spirit of God becomes quenched, He warns. He fires a shot across the bow. His goal is not withdrawal but correction. The way He does this is subtle. You begin sensing something in the atmosphere. A slight shift. A shining. A disturbance in the weight of God in the room. Revival atmospheres rarely collapse suddenly. They first begin to thin.

When I inquired of the Lord regarding what I was feeling, He revealed something surprising. Our worship had slowly become more methodical than relational. We were serving God, but it seemed it was just something "we had to do." Our people were excellent, but we had slowly and unknowingly slipped into a ministry mode that was more about serving people than seeking His face. Both are necessary, but one is more necessary.

When He confirmed what I was sensing, I repented immediately. I did not want that atmosphere to continue. This led me to the second step. I knew I had to address my concerns and personal issues with the church. Every Monday night, we gather to pray. Earlier that day I sent an email and text message to our congregation asking them to make a special effort to attend that evening's prayer meeting. That night, the attendance at our prayer meeting was large; people came eager to pray, but also curious about what the Lord was saying.

That night, I stood before the church and confessed some issues within my heart. I admitted that I had grown familiar with His glory. I had witnessed so many miracles that I had become less moved by them. This grieved the Holy Spirit. Then I asked a question: "Has anyone else felt this?" Hands went up everywhere. The room filled with conviction. People came to the front and knelt at the altar. Repentance spread throughout the room. It was amazing to see the honesty and brokenness.

And suddenly the atmosphere shifted and the room was reset. The presence of God returned in sweetness and power. What was the uneasy feeling I felt prior to our prayer meeting? It was God sounding an alarm. *"Seek My face"* again (Psalm 27:8 NKJV).

WHAT HAPPENS IF WE DO NOTHING?

When pastors or leaders ignore or are slow to respond to divine correction, the spiritual consequences are tangible. In my experience with the manifest presence of the Holy Spirit, Jesus gradually withdraws from services, thus diminishing the "weight of God" in the room. This directly affects the demonstration of God's power, which appears restrained or held back. Miracles, salvations, and transformations will happen, though on a less frequent basis. The intensity of the encounters also declines. The supernatural atmosphere becomes restrained.

Here is the most dangerous part of it all—church activity continues, meetings go on, songs are sung, and sermons are preached, but something sacred has quietly left the room. Chinese Christian church leader Watchman Nee understood this reality when he wrote:

"The Holy Spirit does not shout when He is displeased. He simply becomes quiet. And many never notice when He has withdrawn."[57]

This moment in revival is critical. It is here that the leadership team gets to determine what the next move will be for them as a church and for the work of God. Will they ignore the warning? Or, will they respond accordingly?

Delay is dangerous to revival. Our prompt response to the slightest whisper of the Holy Spirit is paramount. When God's breath ever so slightly touches your ear, everything must pause. Stop everything and listen. What comes next can and will change everything. We must tend to the atmosphere and guard the flame of revival.

One of the clearest pictures of revival decline is something most people have experienced: a campfire.

When a fire is first lit, it burns bright and strong. The flames leap high, the heat is intense, and everyone sitting around it feels the warmth. But a fire does not continue burning simply because it once burned well. It must be tended. Wood must be added. Ash must be cleared away. Someone must remain attentive.

If the fire is neglected, something subtle begins to happen. The flames do not vanish immediately. At first, the fire still appears alive. The coals still glow. The warmth can still be felt. But little by little the fire weakens. The flames shrink. The heat fades. Eventually, only embers remain.

No one extinguished the fire. No storm came. No enemy attacked. The fire died because no one tended it.

Revival often fades the same way. The flame that once burned brightly begins to weaken when prayer is neglected, when repentance becomes rare, and when the hunger for God cools. The fire does not die because God withdrew His power. It dies because the altar was no longer tended.

History has proven something unmistakable: revival is not sustained by great preaching, great music, or large crowds. Revival is sustained by a people who refuse to let their hearts belong to anything other than God. Because the Lord whose name is jealous will not share His glory with anyone or anything. And when His people return to Him with undivided hearts, the fire of revival continues to burn.

34

HOW NOT TO GRIEVE THE HOLY SPIRIT

After speaking about the dangers of grieving and quenching the Holy Spirit, an obvious question must now be asked: How do we avoid it? How do we cultivate a relationship with the Spirit that protects His nearness rather than wounds it?

This is more than a good question; it is a necessary one. If revival is sustained or lost at the level of our responsiveness to the Holy Spirit, then learning how to carefully walk with Him becomes more than essential.

But before we answer that question, pause for a moment and consider something remarkable.

God, in His ultimate wisdom, has chosen to work with human cooperation. The omnipotent Spirit of God is not weak, yet He willingly limits His activity in order to partner with His people. This truth is transformational and should cause us to reflect on what part we are playing in His activity on earth.

In addition, God possesses unlimited power, but He is also gentle and long-suffering. He longs to be loved, welcomed, honored, and responded to. He does not force intimacy; He invites it.

That means our posture toward Him matters.

The following are several ways we can actively guard our relationship with the Holy Spirit and avoid grieving Him.

1. Guard your heart. Your heart is the center of your spiritual life. Everything flows from it. Proverbs 4:23 (NKJV) says, *"Keep your heart with all diligence, for out of it spring the issues of life."* The Holy Spirit does not simply interact with our behavior; He interacts with our hearts. When the heart becomes cluttered with distractions, divided loyalties, or hidden sin, the nearness we once enjoyed with Him begins to weaken. Guarding the heart means continually removing whatever competes for the affection that belongs to God.

2. Guard your mind. The mind is where decisions are formed and directions are chosen. It is the ultimate battleground and often determines if we walk in freedom and power. Romans 12:2 (NKJV) instructs us, *"And do not be conformed to this world, but be transformed by the renewing of your mind, that you may prove what is that good and acceptable and perfect will of God."* Many people grieve the Spirit long before their actions reveal it. It begins in the mind, when worldly thinking replaces spiritual thinking and when God's voice is slowly drowned out by competing voices. A renewed mind keeps us aligned with the Spirit's leadership.

3. Just say "yes." One of the simplest and most powerful ways to walk with the Spirit is learning to say yes quickly. This is essential in walking in the Spirit. Jesus says in John 10:27 (NKJV), *"My sheep hear My voice, and I know them, and they follow Me."* The secret to intimacy with the Holy Spirit is not complicated; it is responsiveness. Every time He prompts you to pray, obey, forgive, give, repent, serve, or speak, a quick "yes" strengthens the relationship. Delayed obedience slowly dulls spiritual sensitivity.

4. Submit to the sanctifying work of the Spirit. Sometimes the Spirit is grieved not because of rebellion, but because of quiet resistance. You cannot continue to please Him without refinement. First Thessalonians 5:23 (NKJV) says, *"Now may the God of peace Himself sanctify you completely; and may your whole spirit, soul, and body be preserved blameless at the coming of our Lord Jesus Christ."* Sanctification is the Spirit's lifelong work of refining us into the image of Christ. At times, this work is uncomfortable because it exposes attitudes, habits, and affections that must change. But every surrendered adjustment deepens intimacy with Him.

5. Walk humbly. Humility attracts the presence of God. Micah 6:8 (NKJV) reminds us, *"He has shown you, O man, what is good; and what does the Lord require of you but to do justly, to love mercy, and to walk humbly with your God?"* Pride resists the Spirit; humility welcomes Him. A humble heart remains teachable, correctable, and sensitive to the smallest whisper of the Spirit.

6. Just say "no." If saying "yes" to the Spirit strengthens intimacy, then saying no to temptation protects it. James 4:7 (NKJV) declares, *"Therefore submit to God. Resist the devil and he will flee from you."* Every temptation that attempts to redirect your heart away from God must be met with a decisive refusal. A big "NO!" Flirting with temptations is one of the quickest ways to grieve the Spirit.

7. Handle promptly whatever the Spirit reveals. The Holy Spirit speaks through Scripture, conviction, wise counsel, and even our conscience. When He reveals something, our response must be immediate. Be decisive because delayed obedience often becomes disobedience. I have learned this the hard way: one ignored prompting rarely remains isolated; resistance grows easier each time we delay responding to Him.

GRIEVING VERSUS QUENCHING THE SPIRIT

This topic is of such significance that I want to ensure you understand the difference between grieving the Spirit and quenching the Spirit.

Grieving the Spirit

- The relationship we have with the Spirit is wounded.
- We resist correction or refuse to change behavior.
- Neglect of intimacy with the Word and the Father.
- Our hearts slowly become indifferent to the things of God.

Quenching the Spirit

- The work of the Holy Spirit becomes suppressed.
- There is a refusal to repent from revealed sin.
- We ignore the promptings to make things right with others.
- The activity of the Spirit in our lives becomes restricted.

Grieving wounds the relationship while quenching restricts the activity. One leads naturally to the other.

35

DARKEN THE GLORY

The history of revivals from the birth of the New Testament Church to the Pensacola Outpouring and other divine visitations reveals a stark and sobering pattern: they begin with purity, hunger, brokenness, and humility. Shortly thereafter, unprecedented salvations, miracles, and deliverances occur. Then sadly it fades, and far too often collapses under the weight of the pressure and our human frailty.

Revival history shows us something both glorious and terrifying: the same human hearts that host the glory of God can darken it.

Jonathan Edwards was the catalyst and a major spiritual figure in the First Great Awakening.

Edwards warned that spiritual pride, criticism, and unrestrained emotionalism could "darken the glory" and hinder the Spirit's work.

It is my firm conviction that when a genuine revival begins, the Lord intends for it to remain until He comes again. Why wouldn't He want it to continue? It stands to reason if people are getting saved, healed, delivered, and set free, why would God want it to come to an end? He does not.

Revivals do not come to a close because God grows weary of pouring out His Spirit. They cease because God has entrusted humans to manage a divine supernatural visitation from heaven, and human choices significantly impact the revival's effectiveness and duration. Heaven sends the glory, but people decide whether it remains.

The ability to steward what God has entrusted to a church, a people, or a region, is difficult and grows more and more difficult every day. Hosting revival is difficult in its own right, but we also have an adversary, the devil. It is a known fact that satan hates whenever the glory of God touches the earth, and he relentlessly seeks to extinguish the flame. His most effective tactic is rarely open persecution; rather, it is quiet corruption. The evil one works subtly, patiently, and strategically to weaken what God has begun. He attacks the very ones called to host the glory.[58]

Certainly, revival will move and shift from time to time, and adjustments will need to be made. This is a necessity and helps revival stay current and aligned with its purpose. Still, I must say again, it is arduous work to steward a move of the Holy Spirit.

We must remain aware of the sensitivity of the Holy Spirit. And at all costs, we must avoid grieving Him. His manifest presence is not automatic. A.W. Tozer said, "The Holy Spirit will not remain where He is not honored. He does not force His presence upon careless hearts."[59]

Throughout my walk with God, there have been times when I have grieved Him. I felt it. I knew it. What I learned—He doesn't leave suddenly; He waits. He waits to see what our next step(s) will be. He grows quiet. He watches and listens. He desires intimacy and purity. His heart longs for us to honor Him and remain in awe of Him.

On a personal note. I never want Him to fade from our meetings. I never want the air in our sanctuary to become thin. I know what that feels like, and it is awful.

The thought of it terrifies me.

I do not want church or life as usual. My eyes have seen too much, and my ears have heard too much for me to ever be content with what used to be.

I have said this before, but I must say it often—the glory of God seldom departs suddenly; rather, the glory fades in inches. It is a gradual withdrawal; it is a slow dimming of the fire. The music may still be strong. The sermons may still be sound. The schedules may still be full. But something holy is missing. Sadly, due to many reasons, the human vessels called to host His presence often don't even know there has been a shift.

History has proven that revival rarely ends with a dramatic collapse. More often, it ends with quiet substitution. We replace presence with activity, structure for glory, and religion for power.

Ichabod was a name given to a child in reflection of God's glory departing from the children of Israel. Why did the Lord lift His glory from His people? Eli's house still functioned religiously. It kept things moving, and the activities of the house were maintained. Yet, the glory had lifted. (See 1 Samuel 4.)

One of the most tragic positions imaginable is when the glory lifts, and no one recognizes it. This is exemplified in Revelation 3 when Jesus is outside the church knocking on the door, asking to be let back in. Yes, it was tragic that the Head of the Church was outside the building. But what is even more tragic is that the people inside did not even know He was gone. They continued on with their ministry without recognizing His absence.

If that episode unfolded once, we must ask a sobering question: Could it happen again?

The church we should feel most sorry for is not the persecuted church; it is the unaware church. The church that does not know that the glory has departed.

We can no longer assume or pretend that our decisions, lifestyles, and worldviews do not have an impact on our relationship with God. They do, profoundly. The notion that our personal choices do not influence our relationship with Jesus and how He interacts with us is a dangerous illusion. While we are accepted into His family by grace and perfectly loved by Him, this does not mean that He is okay with how we live. Grace secures our relationship with God, but obedience sustains our intimacy with Him.

Due to a misrepresentation of grace, I believe we have actually "disgraced grace." By this, I mean we have distorted the pure purpose of God's grace. I think it is one of the greatest tragedies of the modern Church that has led people to live, in some cases, an unconsecrated life unto the Lord.

God's grace was meant to pardon us, receive us, and accept us as we are. In addition, attached to grace is the power to set us free from all sin. Grace is not a doorway that gives us permission to live comfortably in sin. Grace is not permission to remain unchanged; it is power to become transformed.

Such a distortion fundamentally misrepresents God's true character and the genuine intent of grace. The result is profound spiritual weakness, leaving believers impotent and their words of witness even more powerless. Furthermore, this perspective is deeply offensive to God and grieves the Holy Spirit.

In practical application, the hyper-grace message, either intentionally or unintentionally, taught a generation that God overlooks our personal sin, He is never offended, and never disciplines us for disobedience, and no longer calls us to change or be conformed into the image of Jesus (Romans 8:29).

But true biblical grace says: "I love you the way you are, come to Me (Jesus)." It says, "I empower you to be free." It also says, "Because of my grace I call you to walk pure and holy before Me and the world."

We must maintain our intimacy with Christ in order to keep an uninterrupted expression of His glory. We cannot afford to have the glory of God darkened by our indifference and carnality. There is too much at stake; therefore, we must not mismanage His manifest presence.

36

WHY REVIVALS DIE

Without a doubt, history bears witness to powerful surges of the Holy Spirit—holy fires ignited by God that spread rapidly and altered the spiritual climate of communities and even entire nations. We most commonly call these divine visitations *revivals.*

Scholars typically recognize 20 to 25 major revivals that have significantly influenced regions and, in some cases, the world. These revivals include:

- First Great Awakening (1730s–1760s)—Jonathan Edwards, Charles Wesley, George Whitefield
- Second Great Awakening (1790–1840)—Cane Ridge Camp Meeting, Charles Finney
- Layman's Prayer Revival (1857–58)—Jeremiah Lanphier
- Welsh Revival (1904–1905)—Evan Roberts
- Azusa Street Revival (1906–1909)—William Seymore
- Hebrides Revival (1949–1952)—The Smith sisters, Duncan Campbell
- Argentine Revival (1950s–1990s)—Carlos Anaconda
- Jesus Movement (late 1960s–1970s)—Chuck Smith, Lonnie Frisbee
- Toronto Blessing (1994–2000)—John Arnott
- Brownsville Revival (1995–2000)—John Kilpatrick, Steve Hill

These movements shook churches, transformed communities, ignited missionary fervor, and awakened millions to the reality of God. Yet a haunting question remains: *If God is willing to move so powerfully, why do such fires so often burn out?* This question should trouble every believer who longs to see God move again.

If revival can die, then every generation must ask the sobering question: *What causes the flame to fade?*

Every great move of God, including future awakenings, encounters unique struggles, pressures, and disruptions. We must never forget that the enemy, along with our flesh, is a harsh, fierce contender against the kingdom of God.

All past revivals that have come to an end have provided us with crucial patterns. When examined carefully, they reveal recurring pitfalls that weakened and ultimately diminished powerful spiritual movements. In my research on revival history, I have identified recurring patterns that consistently appear when a move of God begins to decline.

REASONS WHY REVIVALS WEAKEN AND DIE

Nearly every revival throughout history ended for one or a combination of the following reasons. They are not listed in order of importance; each represents a major contributor to the weakening of revival:

1. Fatigue. *Physical and emotional exhaustion among the leaders and people who are carrying the movement.* Revival is glorious, but it is also demanding. Long hours of ministry, constant spiritual warfare, and the weight of leadership can wear down even the strongest individuals. When exhaustion sets in and is allowed to remain, leaders can begin to make poor decisions, lose clarity, and become vulnerable to multiple temptations the enemy will provide.

2. Doctrinal Conflict. *Theological differences and doctrinal conflicts that supersede the simplicity of the movement.* When revival begins, the focus is usually simple and clear. Jesus is exalted, and people are having life-changing encounters with God. But over time, debates can arise over doctrinal issues and factions form. Factions are unhealthy when hosting a move of God, splintering the congregation. There must be room for doctrinal disagreement in a revival. Disputes can divide; however, maturity and focus on the greater work have to prevail. We must live with our differences so that the work of God does not weaken.

3. Offense. *This may be the single greatest threat to an ongoing move of the Holy Spirit.*

Offense poisons the atmosphere of revival. It takes the focus off of Jesus and puts it onto ourselves, our feelings. When allowed to remain, bitterness takes root, unity fractures, and trust dissolves. The Holy Spirit always moves powerfully in an environment of humility, brokenness, and forgiveness. He is attracted to it. But offense creates and cultivates the environment where His presence is grieved.

4. Internal Conflict and Division. *New levels of responsibility create immense pressure among leadership teams.* This can cause conflict at the very top. This brings stress and pressure to perform at a high level. Duncan Campbell, who led the Hebrides Revival, said, "The Spirit of God is sensitive. He will withdraw His manifest presence when pride or disunity is allowed to remain." Revival often grows faster than the structures meant to support it. As the movement expands, expectations rise. If leaders are not deeply unified, these pressures can fracture relationships and weaken the spiritual environment.

5. Lack of Corporate Prayer. *Moves of God begin with fervent prayer and are sustained by even greater prayer.* When prayer ceases to be the highest priority, the spiritual power that birthed the revival begins to diminish. The movement may continue outwardly, but the spiritual engine that sustained it grows weaker. History repeatedly proves that revivals end when the prayer meetings stop.

6. Spirit of Familiarity. *Revival becomes routine.* The extraordinary becomes mundane, and familiarity replaces wonder. At the beginning of a revival, people will travel great distances and rearrange their schedules just to be in the meetings—they don't want to miss anything. What once inspired awe eventually feels normal. When the miraculous becomes expected rather than treasured, hunger fades, and the fire weakens.

7. Emotional Excesses and Fanaticism. *When emotional expressions are left without pastoral guidance, they can create confusion and unnecessary scrutiny that will seek to discredit the genuineness of the movement.* Every true move of God attracts both sincere seekers and those who are immature in their faith. Even well-meaning people can be a conduit of excess and extremism that work against the intent of the Holy Spirit for that particular revival. Without wise leadership to shepherd people through these moments, excesses can damage the credibility of the movement and distract from what God is truly doing. Each participant must submit to the leadership as they steward what God is doing.

8. A Lack of In-Depth Training and Discipleship. *Revivals that fail to establish training structures often struggle to sustain long-term revivals.* Awakening without discipleship creates spiritual infants who experience powerful encounters but lack the maturity to steward them. Movements that invest in both theological instruction and spiritual impartation are far more likely to endure.

9. Pride and Self-Promotion. *Christ must remain preeminent, and all personal agendas must bow low so there is no conflict of interest.* Whenever personal agendas rise within leadership, revival begins to weaken. Pride is one of the most dangerous enemies of revival. The Lord hates it. The moment individuals begin seeking recognition rather than honoring Christ, the focus shifts away from God's glory. The Spirit of God will not compete with human ambition.

10. Lack of Finances. *Revival, while spiritual in nature, also has practical realities.* The facilities must be maintained, and the staff must be supported. In addition, new ministries are being birthed and need to be funded. Many historic revivals faced tremendous financial pressure and became a major reason why they faded. Some moves of God never fulfill their intended purpose. When there is an insufficiency of funds, it won't be long until the revival is halted.

11. Distractions. *The enemy will attempt to divert your focus away from what matters most.* When revival begins, the central pursuit is the presence of God. But over time, administrative demands, public attention, and endless activity can pull leaders away from the primary pursuit—seeking the face of God. When the pursuit of God becomes secondary, revival begins to lose its center. Distractions are a primary tool of the enemy.

There is a delicate dance that the leadership must master when God pours out His Spirit. We long for the full expression of the Spirit, yet at the same time, we must pastor and shepherd what God is doing with wisdom and discernment. The public expression of the Spirit is wonderful, but navigating that expression while discipling people requires maturity and care.

This can get complicated.

Shortly after God visited our church in power and people began coming to our services from around the world, in a passing critique, someone took the liberty to make a statement, "If this were a true move of God, then you would have services every night of the week." This struck me deeply and caused me to pause and ask myself, *Should we have services and immersions every night?*

As I sought the Lord, I never felt pressured by Him to do so. Instead, I sensed the Lord instructing me to listen to Him and discover the rhythm of revival that He wanted for us. In other words, I believed that we should move at the pace He sets, not cater to people's expectations.

I have learned that slowing down to strengthen, train, pray, and rest is not negligence; it is stewardship.

I did not want the revival to be short-lived. I believe the Lord gave us a strategy early on to allow the North Georgia Revival to have longevity. We do not hold revival services every night, but we prepare for hosting His presence six out of the seven days each week.

Our church hosts seven prayer meetings a week. We train our people through KINEO Ministry Training Center, which meets on Tuesdays and Thursdays. Today, there are more than 60 KINEO campuses throughout the nation receiving both academic training and spiritual impartation from the revival hub. Additionally, we gather together on Wednesdays for worship and teaching focused specifically on the spiritual health and growth of our people. This allows our teaching team to feed our people who give and serve the world so generously.

I am convinced these decisions early on have allowed us to sustain the strong work of God He is doing among us. Attention must be given to both the spiritual realities and the practical realities that affect revival. Leading through the shifts and movements of Spirit and Truth is essential—yet historically rare.

Revival is a gift from heaven, but its longevity often depends on the humility and vigilance of those entrusted to steward it.

When God entrusts a people with His presence, the responsibility is immense. The flame must be protected. Each person will have to decide whether they will do whatever is necessary to keep it burning.

37

THE POWER OF MOMENTUM

Momentum is one of those realities that is difficult to define, yet unmistakable to experience. When you have it, you know it. You feel it. Things move forward with less resistance. Progress reinforces itself. What once felt heavy begins to feel possible.

Momentum is the reinforcing cycle of forward movement created when small, consistent actions align with purpose. Like a snowball rolling downhill, intentional motion generates energy, turning modest steps into meaningful progress. Momentum does not eliminate effort, but it reduces friction.

Momentum can work for you, or against you.

There is positive momentum, which carries you toward God's purposes, and negative momentum, which quietly pulls you away from them. Negative momentum rarely announces itself. It drifts. If left unchecked, it slides a person, a church, or a movement away from its intended destination. And once momentum is lost, regaining it requires far more effort than sustaining it. This is why momentum must be guarded, stewarded, and protected.

In the beginning, momentum often feels effortless, even easy. Starting strong is common. Sustaining momentum is rare. There are many factors in sustaining momentum; here is one: *faithfulness.* Faithfulness of the leadership, the congregation, and everyone involved to lean on and depend on the never-ending faithfulness of God and His mercy and grace to build His kingdom on earth as it is in heaven.

Momentum collapses when growth outpaces maturity. As responsibility increases, capacity must increase alongside it, spiritually, emotionally, relationally, and structurally. When capacity fails to grow, momentum becomes fragile.

Momentum also looks different in different seasons. It does not disappear randomly. It is either stewarded or squandered over time. Those who sustain momentum learn to flow with God's timing and adapt to His desires.

There are seasons to advance aggressively and seasons to wait quietly. In God's economy, there are times for pruning, cutting, and removing even good things to make room for greater things. There are seasons of maintenance, rebuilding, and strengthening infrastructure.

I have learned the hard way of the fragility of momentum. If momentum is not governed appropriately and with integrity, the very momentum we seek can become reckless and undisciplined. When emotion replaces discernment, decisions become impulsive, credibility erodes, then momentum is eventually lost.

MOMENTUM AND THE CYCLES OF REVIVAL

Momentum may begin with a seismic encounter or sudden shift, but it is sustained one decision at a time. Some of those decisions are difficult and can even upset people. However, it is the daily, unseen choices that keep the movement moving. Yesterday's "yes" cannot carry today's weight. Each new door of obedience automatically closes competing opportunities. Momentum is preserved when we discern God's door for today and give it our yes.

Most people do not backslide on the Lord or quit being faithful because of one catastrophic failure. They quit because they stop saying yes in small ways. Personal and corporate momentum is built and sustained on daily consent.

Churches and revivals with godly momentum can survive mistakes. Without momentum, even minor setbacks can cause collapse. Carefully stewarded momentum can transform a divine visitation into a lasting movement.

If momentum is sustained through faithful obedience, then the question becomes: what actually preserves that momentum in a move of God? The answer is not activity. It is intimacy.

NEARNESS, NOT NOISE

We've all heard the phrase, usually shouted when panic is rising, and someone needs to look useful: "Don't just stand there, do something!" At the right moment, that's great advice. Action matters. Movement matters. Nobody wants to be the person stacking papers while the building is on fire.

But that slogan is not always wise. In fact, there are moments when it needs to be completely reversed. There are times when the most spiritual, strategic, and courageous thing you can do is not act immediately. The better advice in those moments is this: "Don't just do something, stand there."

When leaders experience the first sprinkles of revival and feel the unusual weight of God's presence, questions inevitably arise: What's next? How long will this last? What do we do now?

I am no expert on revival, but I have learned this much: sustained revival momentum flows from nearness, not noise. Noise is attractive. It always has been. And it is easy, very easy to make. We do this all the time. We promote our meetings, and we schedule the most gifted worship leaders and bands. Social media starts buzzing. Graphics roll out. Announcements multiply. We advertise the next speaker, the next night, the next big moment. The goal is simple: generate enough attention to draw a crowd large enough to validate what we are doing.

And let's be honest, it works. Noise fills rooms. Noise creates excitement. Noise can even imitate momentum. But noise is not presence.

Noise can be manufactured. Nearness cannot. Noise is impressive, fast, and visible. Nearness is quiet, slow, and often unseen. And while noise is easy to produce, it is incapable of sustaining a genuine move of God.

Nearness to God, intimacy with Him, is what carries a movement.

Let me be clear, intimacy requires separation. It requires intention. It requires the discipline to step away from the noise, to shut the door behind you, and to enter the quiet place with God. That kind of isolation is difficult. No one naturally enjoys it. Yet, it is essential if heavenly moments are to be sustained.

One of the fastest ways to lose revival momentum is to value presentation over presence. Momentum is a gift from God, and the quickest way to destroy it is to focus on outcomes while neglecting intimacy with the Holy Spirit. When visibility becomes more important than nearness, momentum quietly begins to erode, even while activity increases.

As pastor of Victory in Christ International, Jim Collins observed, "Sustained momentum depends upon disciplined people, disciplined thought, and disciplined action." The same is true spiritually. Prayer, Scripture reading, confession, and waiting before God are not optional disciplines; they are foundational priorities. There are no shortcuts; momentum in revival requires discipline.

Sustaining momentum is not about doing more and more; it is about doing the right things consistently, especially as seasons shift. We must learn that sitting with the Lord in the closet is not passivity or wasted time—it's preparation. It is where we learn, watch, and listen.

38

DON'T LOOSEN YOUR GRIP

One of the most dangerous moments in any move of God is not the beginning. It is not even the opposition that often follows. The most dangerous moment comes later when the excitement fades, the weight increases, and the people carrying the movement must decide whether they will continue pressing forward or quietly step back.

Revival rarely ends because of an obvious, violent assault from the underworld. More often, it fades quietly, not because people walk away, but because they loosen their grip. They don't abandon the flame; they simply step back from it. They remain nearby, close enough to feel its warmth, but far enough to avoid its weight.

Somewhere between the *thrill of stimulation* and the *cost of sanctification,* the temptation comes softly. It doesn't shout. It whispers, *Take a break. You've done enough. You can rest now.* And that whisper is deadly, not because it sounds rebellious, but because it sounds reasonable. What begins as a pause slowly becomes distance. What feels like wisdom becomes retreat. And before long, the grip that once held tightly begins to relax.

History shows us that most revivals don't die from persecution; they die from fatigue, distraction, and the subtle decision to ease off just a bit.

THE TALLEST MOUNTAIN

The tallest mountain in the world is Mount Everest, standing at 29,031.7 feet, straddling the border of Nepal and the Tibet Autonomous Region of China in the Himalayas. Since 1953, roughly 7,000 climbers have stood on its summit, the highest point on the planet. Yet that number hides a sobering reality: far more have attempted the climb than have ever finished it.

Everest is not conquered in a single heroic moment. It is lost in stages, through exhaustion, complacency, overconfidence, or the decision to stop pushing when the summit is still within reach. Many climbers turn back not because the mountain defeated them, but because the climb demanded more than they were prepared to give.

In 1975, Junko Tabei of Japan, at just 35 years old, became the first woman to reach Everest's summit. She would go on to climb the highest mountain on each of the seven continents, a feat known as the Seven Summits. Her achievement was not the result of raw strength alone, but of endurance, discipline, and the refusal to loosen her grip when conditions were hardest.

Climbing Mount Everest is neither cheap nor easy. Securing a place on an expedition team can cost upward of $50,000, and the journey itself can take as long as ten weeks. Three to six of those weeks are spent simply trekking to base camps, while another four to seven weeks are devoted to climbing the most dangerous sections of the mountain.

Progress is slow. The margin for error is razor-thin.

And despite all the preparation, approximately 35 percent of those who attempt the climb never reach the summit. They turn back somewhere along the way. Yes, they can say they tried, but their story will never be the story of those who pushed through, endured the suffering, and joined the small company, just over 7,000 people in history, who have stood on the roof of the world.

Those climbers added their names to Everest's history not because conditions were favorable, but because they refused to quit when conditions became unbearable. They endured thin air, freezing temperatures, numb fingers, exhaustion, fear, and the relentless temptation to turn back. Everest has no mercy for the casual climber. It demands everything, and exposes anyone who came lightly.

History makers are not defined merely by talent, nor by strength. They are defined by their grip. When others loosen their hold to preserve comfort or safety, they tighten theirs. When retreat seems reasonable, even logical, they press forward. These are the ones who refuse to let go of the rope, because they understand that letting go does not just end the climb, it ends the story.

Sir Edmund Hillary later reflected on his ascent with these sobering words: "It is not the mountain we conquer, but ourselves." The final battle on Everest is never with ice or stone; it is with the voice that whispers, "You've gone far enough." Those who silence that voice, who refuse to listen to it, are the ones who make history.

Every day, people quit. It is simply a fact of life. Some walk away from jobs. Others from marriages, teams, callings, or educational pursuits. Rarely do people quit at the beginning, when everything is new, exciting, and full of promise. And rarely do they quit at the end, when the reward is clearly in sight. Most people quit in the middle.

When do runners drop out of a race? In the middle.

When do most students leave college? In the middle.

The reason, in my opinion, is simple: the middle gets heavy. It always does. You are not at the beginning, and the end is not quite in sight. Somewhere along the journey, things shift. What once felt exhilarating now feels demanding. Responsibilities increase, pressure mounts, and progress slows.

In the middle, there are ups and downs, delays, disappointments, and varying degrees of frustration. This is where the cost becomes clear, and the novelty wears off. Simplicity gives way to complexity. And for many, the weight of the middle convinces them that letting go feels not only easier but wiser than holding on.

Each of us must decide how we are going to navigate that weight. The weight is unavoidable, but how we respond to it is not.

I have come to this conclusion: hosting and stewarding a genuine move of God is one of the most demanding responsibilities a person or a church can ever carry. Why? Because in revival, nothing is neutral. Every action matters. Every decision carries weight. There are no private choices when God is moving publicly.

The impact of our decisions never rests on us alone. What we say, how we say it, what we tolerate, and what we pursue ripple outward, touching families, shaping the culture of the church, influencing the community, and affecting countless lives that have been drawn into the orbit of what God is doing.

In a season of revival, words build or wound. Choices either protect the flame or quietly starve it of oxygen. Opportunities and conflicts alike must be weighed carefully and handled with uncommon wisdom, humility, and restraint.

The fire of God that births revival is rarely extinguished in a dramatic moment. More often, it dims slowly. It fades not because God withdraws, but because people gradually stop moving forward with Him. Somewhere along the way, a subtle declaration is made, sometimes out loud, more often in the heart: "This is far enough." The race feels finished. The grip loosens. The pursuit slows.

And this is where history has been decided again and again.

Those who sustain revival are not the most gifted or the most visible, but the most faithful. They are the ones who refuse to let go when the climb is steep, when the air is thin, and when retreat feels reasonable. They understand that holy fire must be carried forward, not merely celebrated. Revival is not sustained by intensity alone, but by endurance, by people who choose, again and again, to keep saying yes.

So hear this as both a warning and an invitation: do not loosen your grip. What God has entrusted to you is worth the cost. You have come too far to let go now. Do not let go of the plow. I know the climb is demanding, but the summit is sacred. And those who hold fast, who steward carefully, walk humbly, and stay aligned with Him, will not only experience revival, but they will help carry it further than it has ever gone before.

They are the ones who will make history.

May we be found among those who held on.

NOTES

1 "Weird Babel of Tongues," *Los Angeles Times,* April 18, 1906.
2 Cecil M. Robeck Jr., *The Azusa Street Mission and Revival: The Birth of the Global Pentecostal Movement* (Nashville: Thomas Nelson, 2006), 1-5.
3 Frank Bartleman, *How Pentecost Came to Los Angeles* (Los Angeles: Frank Bartleman, 1925), 60-61.
4 Allan Anderson, *An Introduction to Pentecostalism: Global Charismatic Christianity* (Cambridge University Press, 2004), 38-42.
5 Vinson Synan, *The Century of the Holy Spirit: 100 Years of Pentecostal and Charismatic Renewal* (Thomas Nelson, 2012).
6 Frank Bartleman, *How Pentecost Came to Los Angeles: As It Was in the Beginning* (Privately Published, 1925), 60-63.
7 https://worldpopulationreview.com/countries/births-per-day.
8 Ibid.
9 https://www.verywellmind.com/what-is-uninvolved-parenting-2794958.
10 https://www.eatrightpro.org/about-us/for-media/press-releases/60-percent-of-foods-purchased-by-americans-contain-technical-food-additives.
11 Charles H. Spurgeon, *The Metropolitan Tabernacle Pulpit,* vol. 10, sermon no. 598, "The Jealous God" (London: Passmore & Alabaster, 1864), 557-558.

12 Duncan Campbell, *The Price and Power of Revival* (Edinburgh: Faith Mission, 1952), 6.
13 J. Edwin Orr, *The Flaming Tongue: The Impact of Twentieth Century Revivals* (Moody Press, 1973), 21.
14 Charles Finney, *Lectures on Systematic Theology* (A.S. Barnes, 1846), 354.
15 Leonard Ravenhill, *Why Revival Tarries* (Bethany House, 1959), 112.
16 Charles Spurgeon, *Morning and Evening* (London: Passmore & Alabaster, 1866), January 25 entry.
17 Duncan Campbell, *The Price and Power of Revival* (Edinburgh: Faith Mission, 1952), 27.
18 Vance Havner, *Revival Comes to Those Who Care* (Fleming H. Revell, 1970), 74.
19 International Health, Racquet & Sportsclub Association, 2023 IHRSA Global Report: The State of the Health Club Industry (IHRSA, 2023).
20 Christopher Bader, Joseph Baker, L. Edward Day, and Ann Gordon, *Chapman University Survey of American Fears 2023* (Chapman University, 2023).
21 Oswald Chambers, *My Utmost for His Highest* (Dodd, Mead & Co., 1935), 189.
22 Leonard Ravenhill, *Why Revival Tarries* (Bethany House, 1959), 97.
23 James K. Hoffmeier, *Ancient Israel in Sinai: The Evidence for the Authenticity of the Wilderness Tradition* (Oxford University Press, 2005), 152-155.
24 John A. Beck, *The Holy Land for Christian Travelers* (Baker Academic, 2017), 56-57.
25 Walter C. Kaiser Jr., *The Old Testament Documents: Are They Reliable and Relevant?* (InterVarsity Press, 2001), 99-101.
26 K.A. Kitchen, *On the Reliability of the Old Testament* (Eerdmans, 2003), 264-266.
27 Stephen Sulkin, "Larval and Juvenile Growth in Decapod Crustaceans," in *The Biology of Crustacea*, vol. 2, ed. D.E. Bliss (Academic Press, 1983), 11-20.

28 Carl Wilson, interview by Maine Department of Marine Resources, in *Maine Lobster Research Program Annual Report* (Maine DMR, 2017), comment on molting vulnerability.

29 Jerome A. Jackson, "Molting Patterns and Renewal in Bald Eagles," *Journal of Raptor Research* 24, no. 4 (1990): 154-160.

30 *Newzoo,* Global Gamer Study 2023.

31 *Entertainment Software Association,* "2023 Essential Facts About the U.S. Video Game Industry" (ESA, 2023).

32 *Limelight Networks,* State of Online Gaming Report 2022.

33 Jane McGonigal, *Reality Is Broken: Why Games Make Us Better and How They Can Change the World* (Penguin, 2011).

34 *Barna Group,* "Most Americans Believe in Heaven…but Not Hell," April 13, 2016, https://www.barna.com/research/most-americans-believe-in-heaven-but-not-hell/.

35 Dennis F. Kinlaw, *This Day with the Master: 365 Daily Meditations* (Francis Asbury Press, 2002), November 14.

36 Derek Prince, *They Shall Expel Demons: What You Need to Know About Demons—Your Invisible Enemies* (Chosen Books, 1998), 141.

37 Charles G. Finney, *Lectures on Revivals of Religion* (Fleming H. Revell, 1868), 57.

38 T. Desmond Alexander, *From Eden to the New Jerusalem: An Introduction to Biblical Theology* (Kregel, 2008), 21-22.

39 "John Stephen Akhwari," *Olympedia;* https://www.olympedia.org/athletes/76535.

40 Duncan Campbell, *Hebrides Revival-2* (transcript of 1968 message on the Hebrides Revival), tape message, "Hebrides Revival," Revival Library archive.

41 R.T. Kendall, "8 Observations on the Hebrides Revival," *Ministry Today,* June 23, 2019, https://www.premierchristianity.com/home/rt-kendall-8-observations-on-the-hebrides-revival/2176.article.

42 Charles G. Finney, *Lectures on Revivals of Religion* (Leavitt, Lord & Co., 1835), 30.

43 Michael L. Brown, *Authentic Fire: A Response to John MacArthur's Strange Fire* (Destiny Image Publishers, 1999), 281-285.

44 Michael L. Brown, *From Holy Laughter to Holy Fire* (Destiny Image Publishers, 1996), 198-201.

45 Duncan Campbell, *The Lewis Awakening 1949–1953* (Edinburgh: The Faith Mission, 1954), 14-15.

46 A.W. Tozer, *Reclaiming Christianity* (Christian Publications, 1985), 62-63.

47 https://www.redfin.com/news/vacant-homes-sell-for-less-money/?utm_source=chatgpt.com.

48 Martyn Lloyd-Jones, *Darkness and Light: An Exposition of Ephesians 4:17-5:17*, pages 264-277.

49 Leonard Ravenhill, *Why Revival Tarries* (Bethany House, 1959), 25.

50 Frank Bartleman, *Azusa Street* (Frank Bartleman, 1925), 78.

51 Frank Bartleman, *Azusa Street* (Frank Bartleman, 1925).

52 Francis Chan, *Crazy Love* (David C. Cook, 2008), 64.

53 A.W. Tozer, *The Knowledge of the Holy* (Harper & Row, 1961), 111.

54 Duncan Campbell, *The Lewis Awakening* (Edinburgh: Banner of Truth, 1974), 78.

55 Andrew Murray, *The Spirit of Christ* (Whitaker House, 1998), 145.

56 John Owen, *The Holy Spirit* (Banner of Truth, 1998), 214.

57 Watchman Nee, *The Release of the Spirit* (Christian Fellowship Publishers, 1965), 51.

58 A.W. Tozer, *The Pursuit of God* (Christian Publications, 1948), 104.

59 Ibid.

ABOUT TODD SMITH

Todd Smith and his wife, Karen, have served as the senior pastors of Christ Fellowship Church for 16 years. Along with serving in pastoring roles for more than 35 years, Pastor Todd has preached the gospel, led crusades, traveled to the mission fields, and participated in pastors' conferences in more than 28 countries around the world, as well as hosting the outbreak of the North Georgia Revival that began February 11, 2018. Pastor Todd and Karen are currently traveling worldwide, spreading revival fire wherever they minister.

From

Todd Smith

The nations are in an uproar. It seems like daily the world is plunging deeper and deeper into sin, crisis, and turmoil. Maybe this picture describes your life. Maybe you're feeling discouraged, hopeless, or just longing for something morein your life and something fresh in your walk with God.

Be encouraged and lift up your head. Revival is at hand!

In this one-of-a-kind devotional, Pastor Todd Smith of the North Georgia Revival and pastor of Christ Fellowship Dawsonville, GA has assembled together leaders from many streams-both the generals of revival and those whose names you may not know yet, but they are on the frontlines of global moves of God. Every entry will stir your faith to believe that you too can experience the fresh fire of revival in your life because each author writes from the place of authority. They've seen God move powerfully and want you to know that it's possible for you to experience Him too!

Featuring 70 powerful and inspirational mini-chapters, Igniting Revival Fire Everyday will surely ignite your heart daily to go deeper in your relationship with God, usher you into fresh encounters with the Holy Spirit, and radically inspire your faith to believe that revival is possible. In your city and nation. In your household and workplace. In your family, marriage, and among your children. In your own heart and walk with God!

Purchase your copy wherever books are sold

From

Todd Smith

Become a Resting Place For God's Presence and Power!

Historically, God has moved mightily through revivals, awakenings, and outpourings of His Spirit. But these legendary moments are only a glimpse into what God desires for you each and every day.

Your everyday life can be a permanent dwelling place for God's presence.

Todd Smith, pastor of Christ Fellowship Dawsonville and leader of the North Georgia Revival, has firsthand experience in creating a habitation for God. He was on the verge of quitting the ministry when the Holy Spirit began showing him how to create a place in his life for the presence of God to live.

Discover the supernatural power and peace that comes when you make your life a habitation for God's glory!

Purchase your copy wherever books are sold

In the Right Hands, This Book Will Change Lives!

Most of the people who need this message will not be looking for this book. To change their lives, you need to **put a copy of this book in their hands.**

Our ministry is constantly seeking methods to find the people who need this anointed message to change their lives. **Will you help us reach these people?**

Extend this ministry by sowing three, five, ten, or *even more* books today and change people's lives for the better! Your generosity will be part of catalyzing the Great Awakening that many have been prophesying and praying for.